Spiritual Truth
Using the Enneagram

By Alan Fensin

Spiritual Truth Using the Enneagram

Published by
**Way Enterprises Division
Burlington National Inc.**
Box 732
Metairie, LA 70004

Copyright © 1995 by Alan Fensin
All rights reserved. No part of this book may be reproduced, stored in a retrieval system, or transmitted in any form or by any means, electronic, mechanical, photocopying, recording, or otherwise, without prior written permission of the publisher.

Printed in the United States of America.

Library of Congress Catalog Card Number: 95-090268

ISBN 0-9622183-3-2

Contents

Introduction   7

Chapter 1 The Enneagram   13
- Why the Enneagram?   15
- The Quick View   19
- The Nine Enneagram Personalities   21
- # 1 Perfectionist   24
- # 2 Helper   27
- # 3 Achiever   30
- # 4 Unique   33
- # 5 Observer   36
- # 6 Loyalist   39
- # 7 Optimist   42
- # 8 Champion   45
- # 9 Peacemaker   48
- Growth   51
- Growth for # 1   52
- Growth for # 2   54
- Growth for # 3   55
- Growth for # 4   57
- Growth for # 5   59
- Growth for # 6   61
- Growth for # 7   62
- Growth for # 8   64
- Growth for # 9   65

Chapter 2 Additional Enneagram Information   67
- Overview   69
- History of the Enneagram   70
- Enneagram Theory   72
- The Three Groups   72
- Triangle Symbol   73
- The Symbol with Three Groups   74
- The Enneagram Symbol   76
- Movement Along the Lines   77

- Dominant Wing — 79
- Understanding Others — 82
- Physical Characteristics — 82
- Numbers That Could Look Similar — 85

Chapter 3 The Great Religions — 87
- Overview — 89
- Why a Spiritual Quest? — 90
- Proofs of God — 91
- Why a Religion? — 92
- Common Elements of Religions — 93
- The Great Living Religions — 96
- Hinduism — 98
- Buddhism — 104
- Taoism — 112
- Judaism — 117
- Islam — 124
- Christianity — 129
- Spiritual Choices and Practices — 138
- Spiritual Healing — 143
- Spiritual Decision — 145

Chapter 4 Spiritual Fulfillment — 147
- Overview — 149
- Spiritual Meditations — 152
- One Year Spiritual Training — 153
- Reality — 148
- I am — 158
- One God — 162
- Love — 165
- Trust — 166
- Error — 167
- Forgiveness — 175
- Love–Peace — 181
- Abundance — 185
- Present — 186
- Prayer — 187
- Listen — 190
- Purpose — 191
- Healing — 194
- One — 195

• Teacher	196
• Daily Meditations	197
• Recovery Work	198

Enneagram Resources   199
About the Author   200

Acknowledgments

I would like the thank the following people for their help on this book:

- **Wendy Zaritsky** for her help in major editing of sections of this book.
- Lolita Roy, Peggy Gelpi, Michelle Guirard, Elizabeth Fensin, Severine Singh, Leslie Fensin, and Hal Cohen for their help and contributions.

Introduction

<u>Spiritual Truth</u> is so named because it offers the information needed for the individual to understand their true self and unfold into a lifetime of peace and holiness.

Introduction

This book is a journey intended to increase your understanding that spiritual truth has appeared in many ways throughout the history of humanity. Only the form, flavor and content of the transmission of spiritual truth has changed. The culture, historical context, and individual skew of the recorders of these truths is what is different in each religion. But Truth stands behind all the interpretations.

In the West, we have come to think, like all cultures, that **our** way of viewing the world is **the** way everyone perceives it. In fact, our view is myopic and peculiar to our "skew." Our personality or ego, wants us to believe that the foundations of our belief systems or religions are correct and that there can only be **one** truth, which is **our** truth. From the study of the Enneagram, we can begin to understand that we all see things differently, based on our personality type and also our level of mental health and spiritual development.

Thus the Enneagram of Personality Types can become for us a powerful tool for not only healing and transforming ourselves, but it can transform and heal our understanding of others and the world around us.

We are all part of one gigantic human family, and as we move along our path we can come to see more of the unity and parallels between all things and in all religious and spiritual paths.

All religions were formed as the result of the recording of spiritual experiences and events by Teachers and students. Each individual who recorded their impressions layered and often obscured the truth of their Teacher by the placement of their bias, or fixation onto them. By using the tool of the Enneagram of Personality Types, we can apply our Self-Observation to see these truths more objectively and fully.

Our journey must always begin with ourselves, since the only place change, healing and transformation can truly take place is in the present moment through our own efforts. Understanding is the bridge to creating a new, richer, spiritualized world both inside of us and in the world around us. All efforts we make to study spiritual traditions and religions will be effort well spent towards expanding our understanding of spiritual truth.

In his book, <u>Motivation and Personality</u> Abraham Maslow categorizes human needs into seven levels, known as *Maslow's Need Hierarchy*. The seven levels encompass physiological needs such as food and shelter, the very basic needs; needs for shelter and security, sex, love, and acceptance; the need for worth and esteem; and finally, the need for knowledge about life and God. Therefore, it seems that to achieve wholeness, we must determine a proper and practical way of satisfying each of these categories of needs, including the need for spiritual beliefs and practices.

Since the advent of rapid global communications, many religious paths have opened to us. There are hundreds of therapies for the body and for the mind; religions and cults for the spirit. How can we make an educated choice? How can we know what will work for us?

Most of us bounce through life haphazardly, guided by our likes and dislikes and our old familiar patterns. We are influenced by advertisements and by our friends in our choices of habits and activities. What if we could be truly and impartially informed – even in a general way – about the choices available to us in our spiritual unfoldment?

This book aims to give such information and choices: information about choices to grow at the spiritual level.

<u>*Spiritual Truth Using the Enneagram* *contains four parts:*
- *The Enneagram*
- *Additional Enneagram Information*
- *The Great Religions*
- *Spiritual Fulfillment*</u>

With this book, each one of us can build his or her own unique system by choosing the most appropriate elements from among the many options available. The key here is informed choices. *Spiritual Truth Using the Enneagram* offers general yet comprehensive information about the many elements of our psychological and spiritual lives. By studying the Enneagram of Personality Types and the world's religions, we can create a bridge to new understanding and a broader, more objective world view.

But of course in the end, the choice remains yours. We each travel a very unique path on this earth and we must each take full responsibility for achieving the optimum results with the gifts we have received. Choosing the right plan for a lifetime can lead you to wholeness and holiness.

CHAPTER 1
THE ENNEAGRAM

> *"To escape from prison the first thing you must recognize is that you are in prison. Otherwise, no escape is possible."*
> — *George Gurdjieff*

Overview of the Chapter

Why the Enneagram of Personality Types is a powerful tool for personal and spiritual development.

This chapter is about psychological growth. Growing in psychological self awareness is a necessary step for a grounded spiritual awakening. Otherwise the lower aspects of the personality will keep one unaware of higher truths.

One tool that sheds light on our personality is called the Enneagram. It represents a tool that dramatically advances self observation. It allows us to individually make a spectacular breakthrough in our self understanding. It's also a very accessible psychological model that most people can easily understand.

The Enneagram teaches a clear method of letting go of the personality's limited world view and opening up to the gifts of sacred wisdom.

Every spiritual quest starts with the questioning of generally accepted beliefs about who we really are. The Enneagram of Personality Types will show us that we waste much of our life energy defending a false self-image that is not really who we are. Our true Self is spiritual in nature and infinitely greater than our false-self.

The Enneagram can provide an opening in our lives that can lead to a deepening of spiritual wisdom. The Enneagram shows us how our primary personality limitation was created as the core of our personality. Once we become aware of our limiting biases towards life, we can then more easily experience the full, 360 degree spectrum of possibilities and world views.

> *Great people usually have one thing in common – a deep knowledge of themselves.*

In our mother's womb we each felt safe and secure, without worry or anxiety. Very early during the first year of our lives we begin to feel separate and we begin to lose our total trust in life. We begin to experience various needs and desires that were no longer fulfilled.

In our quest to satisfy our needs, we learned to modify our natural behavior. These behavioral changes that we thought would bring the fulfillment of our needs and desires then become part of our emerging personality. These behavior modifications are normal and essential in helping us survive childhood. Still, with time our identification with this modified behavior becomes so strong that we forget our true Self and instead identify with this learned behavior.

As adults, our childhood decisions now determine our automatic responses. Our attention is controlled by an unending succession of desires and fears that keep us from knowing our true Self. An important part of deepening spiritual life is understanding these automatic responses. These automatic controls are described by the Enneagram and turn out to be the very thing that keeps us from spiritual growth.

Another value of understanding the Enneagram of Personality Types is the realization that there are other objective measures for truth beyond our own individual perception of how things are. There are in fact nine different and distinct viewpoints of how things really are. Once we recognize that there are other equally valid ways of seeing things it opens up a new tolerance in our dealing with the rest of humanity.

> *People don't see things as **they** are. They see things as **they** are.*

What is the Enneagram?

The Enneagram of Personality Types is a tool for spiritual development with its roots in ancient Middle Eastern wisdom. It is a psychological system based on nine fundamental personality patterns that effect our beliefs and behaviors. The Enneagram is a powerful system that can increase our understanding of the mechanism of our individual personality type.

> *The Enneagram is a system for observing ourselves and increasing our psychological clarity.*

Today, in the modern world. we don't have the opportunity to be trained with the initiation rights that our ancestors used. These initiation rights showed us that we were not the center of the world. The student had to give up control to the elders. This allowed the students, who once thought they were the center of the universe, to emerge with a larger world view. They were then part of the whole group.

The Enneagram can serve in much the same way by showing us how we fit into this personality system. People typically think along the lines of **my story** or **their story**. With knowledge and understanding of the Enneagram system, we can see a much larger picture and can then think in terms of the **whole story**. Understanding the Enneagram produces a direct experience of observing our personality and is not just a belief or a theory.

The Enneagram also gives individual instructions on how to use this information to rise above our limitations and develop our higher potential. Study of the Enneagram increases our self-awareness and principles of spiritual truth.

The first step to freedom from the control of our psychological Self is to recognize that the personality that we commonly call our Self is not our true Self. The Enneagram calls it the false Self. If we understand the limitations of our false Self we can then drop these limitations. Then we can chose to live less out of limiting automatic behavior, and more in the fullness of reality. This gives us the freedom to discover our true spiritual identity.

Most personal growth programs treat all personalities the same way. This limits their usefulness for many people. The power of the Enneagram comes from individual guidance for individual personalities. For example. a serious personality may be instructed to lighten up; while a scattered personality may be instructed to get more serious.

There are an infinite number of different and distinct personalities, just as there are an infinite number of points on a circle. We can divide the circle of a compass into North, South, East, and West. Similarly we can divide the infinite number of personalities into nine basic directions or chief personality features. These nine personality types are the basis of the Enneagram system.

Due to the nature of the Enneagram, both positive and negative aspects of each personality are examined, but the Enneagram is not intended to pass judgment on anyone. Each personality number has different strengths and weaknesses, but in the final analysis **there is no personality number that is any better than any other.** There are, however, nine different basic types of personalities. Each has the potential for spiritual redemption and freedom from the personality's prison.

This chapter begins with a quick view of each Enneagram personality type, followed in the next section by a more extensive description. Next is the section on guidelines for growth for each personality type. This is followed by a section on determining the personality types of others, and finally Chapter 2 concludes with information on the theory and history of the Enneagram.

The Quick View of the Enneagram

It's easiest to begin the determination of your personality type by reading the nine short statements below. Many people can narrow the choices to one or two possibilities just from this quick view. However, it is still recommended that you read the more detailed descriptions in the next section to verify your determination of type.

Type 1. The perfectionist do what they think is the right thing. They are upright, fastidious and honest. They act on their own values as long as they believe they are in the right. They are careful and excel at meticulous tasks that don't necessarily require speed. They can have a good sense of humor about themselves, such as in the style of Johnny Carson. They generally hold their own ground around issues of moral principle.

Type 2. The helper is sensitive to what others want, and they are care takers of others. Twos are very empathic and sensitive to feelings. Relationships are their main concern or preoccupation. Twos often have a charming sense of silliness and playfulness in the style of Goldie Hawn. Twos know how to impress others, and they generally know how to get people to like them.

Type 3. The achiever is enthusiastic, competitive, hard working and give themselves over to a job or task, with one-hundred percent of their effort. They are goal or results oriented. Threes mingle and mix well in any group they choose. Threes know how to present an image that is desirable. They have a keen awareness of the image that they present to the world.

Type 4. The unique personality has a highly developed artistic sense. They can be melancholic and are intensely in touch with deep feelings and the sadness and pain of existence. Fours tend to be good artists of all kinds, acting, painting, singing, writing etc. They know what dramatic effect is and how to use it. They know how to make an entrance or exit. They have a good sense of style and fashion. They will express themselves as individuals.

Type 5. The observer has a good sense of objectivity. They are aware of the value of things and the limitations of time and money. Fives minimize their needs and are efficient in their use of those resources at their disposal. They are independent and don't look to others to take care of them. Fives can be good listeners. They will not usually rock the boat or stir up trouble. Fives are often emotionally detached and tend to observe life without really participating in it.

Type 6. The loyalist tends to focus on the things that could go wrong. They are dutiful and loyal and know who has the power in a group. They have a long attention span and can really be very logical about the things they are doing. They are good at planning and implementing strategies. They are adventurous and take risks. Sixes can be rebellious in a positive way. They sometimes question authority, stand up to authority, and take an opposing point of view. They can confront and question.

Type 7. The optimist can be charming and easy to get along with. They don't appear to have many problems and are generally optimistic, pleasant and sociable. They can be intellectuals. Sevens have dreams and visions of what's possible. They often have discriminating gourmet tastes in food, clothing and other things in life. They have a positive, upbeat approach to life. They are good idea people and imaginative brainstormers.

Type 8. The Champion is powerful and readily lets people know where they stand with them. What you see is what you get. They do not have a problem confronting things in their life. They focus on issues of their strength and other's weakness. They can be really good friends. In general they do not play mind games. They can be defenders of the weak. Beneath the hard outer shell of the Eight is a soft, gentle, vulnerable heart.

Type 9. The peacemaker is easy to be with and sees all sides of an issue. If they are umpires in a ball game they could decisively call ball or strike. Nines usually do the right thing instinctively without thinking about it. They are fairly generous and easy going. Nines are warm and have big hearts. They are there for others and don't appear to expect anything in return.

The Nine Enneagram Personalities

The following sections give a more detailed description of each of the nine personality types.

Other Personality Names That Have Been Used for This Personality Type

Each personality number is given a name that describes the central aspect or pre-occupation of the personality. It is followed by several other names that have also been used.

Key to the Personality

Each of the nine personalities **excessively fear and resist** a different aspect in their lives. It is this often hidden resistance that distorts their understand of life and gives rise to their individual personality's skew.
- This fear was a major factor in developing each of the nine personalities.
- This fear has also been called an avoidance, fixation, pre-occupation, compulsion, fundamental addiction, and also a basic life distortion.

Self Definition/Self Image

Each personality views themselves in a unique way.

Personality Traits

Next are a list of typical personality attributes with various characteristics that are believed to be common to each personality type.

Unlike other psychological systems, the Enneagram of Personality Types is based on our motivation – not on our behavior. Often two individuals' behavior could appear to be the same, yet it is driven by different motivators. Consequently, one does not have to exhibit every personality trait in the list to still be that personality number.

Preoccupations
Certain activities and motivation are of concern to each personality type.

Common Occupations
For each Enneagram personality type certain occupations are more typical than others. People usually select the occupation which is most suited to their personality. However, this is not always true, so use this section as just another indicator.

Method of Communication
Different personalities naturally communicate in different ways. What they have to say and how they say it are valuable indications of their Enneagram number.

Examples of Famous People
The names given in these sections were selected because a number of Enneagram teachers have agreed that these were good examples of the personality type.

Examples of International Enneagrams
The cultures of various countries reflect basic Enneagram personality traits. This does not mean that everyone in that country is a certain personality. It does however indicate that the overall tendencies of the national culture leans towards a particular personality number. This is another way to understanding the Enneagram.

Animals
This is another useful concept to assist understanding of the different personalities.

Typical Family History
Our individual genetics certainly influence our personality to a large degree. The situation we are born into also greatly influences the development of our personalities. Enneagram teachers agree that the basic personality is formed prior to age seven. Many believe that it develops much earlier.

Because of genetic predisposition, different children perceive the same set of circumstances differently. The reality of the social environment is filtered and modified by this genetic predisposition. Still, psychological consultants who understand the Enneagram say that their clients usually report similar childhood circumstances corresponding to their Enneagram personality numbers.

Possible Problems

Each personality number views life differently – and consequently has its unique problems, challenges and patterns. However, for each number, the healthier individual will have far fewer of these unhealthy traits.

1 Perfectionist

Other Personality Names That Have Been Used for the Type One Personality
- Inspector
- Resenter
- Reformer
- Corrector
- Judge
- Improver
- Crusader

Key to the One Personality
- Ones excessively fear and resist imperfection in their lives.
- Instead they replace imperfection with a never ending search for perfection.

Self Definition/Self Image
"I am right. I am hardworking."

Personality Traits
- Ones do what they think is the right thing.
- Ones don't like people who break rules.
- They are inclined to see things as right or wrong, black or white.
- Ones can have feelings of being unimportant or worthless.
- Ones often try to reform or improve things.
- Ones keep a tight rein on their emotions.
- Ones often block real feelings with "shoulds and oughts."
- They are careful and excel at meticulous tasks.
- They are usually well organized.
- Ones have strong self-discipline.
- Ones strive to improve their situation.
- Ones are idealistic.
- Ones are people who usually try to do their best.
- They can be critical of themselves and others and have a fierce internal critic.
- Ones have high standards of themselves and others.
- They like to improve things and work hard.

Chapter 1 The Enneagram

- They dread being judged or criticized by others.
- Ones have a cold simmering anger which they seldom allow to boil over.

Preoccupations
- Demanding internal standards.
- Comparing themselves to others.
- Concern with criticism.

Common Occupations
Ones excel in those positions requiring skill, and precision and correct action. They are often employed in the following occupations:
Nurse, preacher, quality control, educator-teacher, accountant, engineer, technician, secretary, auto-mechanic, law enforcement

Method of Communication
Ones communicate by preaching, teaching, and moralizing. They can complain about what is wrong. This is more of an angry complaint to change something and not just resignation at the way things are. There can be an attitude in their conversations that is telling others what to do for their own good.

Examples of Famous Ones
Ann Landers, Nancy Reagan, William F. Buckley, Tom Smothers, Johnny Carson, Dr. Jeckyll (Mr. Hyde is an eight), Barbara Walters, Katherine Hepburn, Confucius, Audrey Hepburn, Tom Brokaw, H. Ross Perot, Harry Truman, Margaret Thatcher, Al Gore.

Examples of International Enneagrams
England and Switzerland are examples of an Enneagram number One countries. They are hard-working and quite proper, generally showing little display of hot anger.

Animals
The terrier, ant, and bee are examples of Ones.

Typical Family History

They usually get their special sense of self from their father. The One child feels ignored on a deep emotional level and usually does not connect with the mother. The psychological message the child received were often "Be good. Behave yourself. Work hard. Don't be childish."

Possible Problems

Number Ones are upset by people who are sloppy about work or appearance. They are easily upset by those who ridicule or criticize them.

Ones have a tendency to believe they are the only people who can do anything right. Consequently, they resent other people whose performance does not meet their high standards. They can become judgmental, unwilling to be wrong, and involved in conflicts. Often Ones are emotionally unable to express their feelings and withhold these feelings instead of dealing with them.

When life is going especially bad, Ones feel misunderstood and have a tendency to be depressed and to withdraw from others. They can feel lost and suffer from self-hate.

2 Helper

Other Personality Names That Have Been Used for the Type Two Personality
- Giver
- Assistant
- Lover
- Nurturer
- Supporter
- Caretaker
- Pleaser

Key to the Two Personality
- Two's overly resist feeling that they have personal needs.
- Instead, they take care of the needs of others, and want to be needed and accepted by others.

Self Definition/Self Image
"I am helpful."

Personality Traits
- Twos are very empathic and sensitive to feelings.
- Twos know how to get people to like them.
- Twos want to love and be loved.
- They can be genuinely caring of others.
- They are usually dependable and can keep their word
- Twos want others to feel welcome and comfortable in their home or work environment.
- They frequently compliment others.
- Twos act more on feelings rather than logic but they can repress feelings in order to be loved.
- They have difficulty recognizing their own needs.
- Twos see relationship as doing for others.
- Twos can be self-sacrificing, giving up their own wants and needs for others..
- Twos take pride in being needed and important in other people's lives.
- Twos are normally caring, empathetic, sensitive and oriented toward helping or saving others.

- Twos are very concerned with what others think of them.
- Twos are generous with their feelings and time and people often seek their comfort.

Preoccupations
- Gaining approval and avoiding rejection.
- Pride in the importance of oneself in relationships.
- Submission to a powerful other person, then identifying with the other person in order to avoid feeling depressed or dealing with themselves.
- Altering oneself to meet the needs of other people.

Common Occupations
Twos excel in positions requiring sympathy and warmth. They are often employed in the following occupations:
Social work, psychologist, physician, nurse, executive-secretary, teacher, minister

Method of Communication
Twos communicate by giving help and advice. They like to talk about other people, their problems and their issues. They usually pay close attention to others while they talk, and often hold eye contact with others. They can also quickly be intimate with your problems.

Examples of Famous Twos
Barbara Bush, Dolly Parton, Goldie Hawn, Sally Field, Elton John, Jerry Lewis, Elvis Presley, Mr. Rogers, Marilyn Monroe, Mother Teresa.

Examples of International Enneagrams
Tibet and the Philippines are example of Enneagram number Two personality countrIes. Their people are helpful and kind.

Animals
A licking puppy is an example of a Two.

Typical Family History

Twos get their special sense of self from their father. This is especially true for female Twos who may have been daddy's special little girl. The child learns to keep the flow of love and attention coming their way with good and often manipulative behavior. Twos perceives that people will like them if they are loving, pleasant, and nice.

Possible Problems

Number Twos are upset by people who do not need their help. Twos resent people who cause them to feel that they are intruding on their privacy. They dislike being ignored or disregarded and hate being unneeded.

Twos tend to believe they do not have needs, so they often project their real needs on to other people and try to help them. In the process Twos may feel they are the victims of life. Twos want people to think of them as helpful and loving, but all the while they are attempting to manipulate other people who may resent them in turn.

If they become mentally unhealthy, Twos have a tendency to want vengeance and control. They may either exhibit aggressive behavior or they may be unable to actually confront their enemies and instead develop physical or mental illnesses in order to get needed attention from others.

3 Achiever

Other Personality Names That Have Been Used for the Type Three Personality
- Succeeder
- Performer
- Motivator
- Administrator
- Marketer

Key to the Three Personality
- Overly resists failure and disgrace.
- Instead, they feel secure by identifying with success.

Self Definition/Self Image
"I am successful. I can accomplish many things."

Personality Traits
- Threes mingle and mix well in any group they choose.
- They like to better and improve their image.
- They seek approval for performance rather than for who they are.
- Threes know how to look good and are image-driven.
- They like recognition and awards.
- They are good at organizing their lives.
- Threes work hard, and give one-hundred percent to their efforts.
- They are almost always busy doing something.
- They set high goals and sustain a high level of productivity.
- Threes present themselves well and make a good first impression.
- They are very goal oriented; they want to finish first.
- They are usually self-assured, cheerful and rarely depressed.
- Threes are concerned with how they appear to others.
- They are practical and efficient people.
- They like to be busy and are sometimes called "doing people" or type "A" personalities.

Preoccupations
- Identification with competitive achievement.
- Constantly adjusting their image in order to present the image that they think is desired.
- Replacement of genuine feelings with the current role they perform.
- Deceiving themselves in order to maintain their sense of image.
- Working on multiple tracks simultaneously.

Common Occupations
Threes excel in positions requiring management or marketing/sales skills. They are often employed in the following occupations:
Marketing, sales, promotion, advertising, banking, entrepreneur, politician, acting, fashion, physician.

Method of Communication
Threes tend to "self-promote" and talk about the great things that are going on in their lives. They will try to enroll you in doing what they are doing. Threes sell themselves. They can have a positive lift at the end of a sentence.

They can speak very fast when they want to deliver a point. They some times say "Ah" to help them hold their turn to speak.

Examples of Famous Threes
President John F. Kennedy, President Jimmy Carter, Arnold Schwartznegger, Werner Erhard, Doris Day, Donald Trump, Robert Redford, Wolfgang Amadeus Mozart, Tom Cruise, Dick Clark, Cybill Shepherd, Bryant Gumbel.

Examples of International Enneagrams
The United States is an example of an Enneagram number Three personality country. It is very success oriented and rejects failure.

Animals
A Chameleon and a Peacock are examples of Threes.

Typical Family History

Threes get their special sense of self from their father, but to a less personal degree than the number Two child. They were prized for what they could produce or achieve rather than for being themselves. The Three child wants the father's special attention but never seemed to quite get it. They therefore go into a performance role that never ends, in their attempt to get the special attention. The Three child doesn't get its special sense of itself because of the person they are but rather for what things they can accomplish or achieve.

Possible Problems

Number Threes become upset with people who find faults with their work or who say they don't work hard enough.

Threes tend to be efficient in getting many tasks completed but they have difficulty dealing with negative results. They compulsively avoid even the possibility of failure or anything else that makes them look bad in front of others.

When life is going especially bad, Threes have a tendency to be out of touch with their emotions and to either become hostile or else to become lazy, "space-out," and operate mechanically.

4 Artist

Other Personality Names That Have Been Used for the Type Four Personality
- Romantic
- Unique
- Creator
- Individualist
- Visionary
- Special person
- Symbol maker

Key to the Four Personality
- They overly resist average or commonplace lives.
- Instead, they embellish their life so that they become unique, special, and authentic.

Self Definition/Self Image
"I am unique and special and do not conform to ordinary standards."

Personality Traits
- Fours are often introspective, aesthetic, and see themselves as different from others.
- They are concerned with analyzing the feelings and motivations of themselves and others.
- Fours can cry easily and can be extremely emotionally affected by sorrow and pain.
- They can be creative and appreciate the beauty of nature.
- Fours often seem to have dramatic events happening around them.
- Fours have difficulty being understood by others.
- They can over react to criticism.
- Fours have a highly developed artistic sense.
- Fours view life as a series of beginnings and endings.
- Fours may be on a quest to find the meaning of life.
- They have a good sense of style and flair.
- Fours are impatient with a mundane and ordinary life..
- They know what dramatic effect is and how to use it.

- They express themselves as individuals.
- They long for some missing ingredient in their life, such as a new lover or other difficult to get desire.

Preoccupations
- Attraction to what is distant and unavailable.
- Attracted to sad or melancholy mood.
- Impatience with ordinary feelings
- Wanting to dramatize feelings through a sense of loss.

Common Occupations

Fours excel in positions in the arts or in something creative. They are often employed in the following occupations:

Acting, dancing, painting , design, interior design, critic, entertainer, therapist, and counselor.

Method of Communication

Fours tell sad stories about their problems and the drama in their lives. They complain in a resigned way and with a sadness in their voice. Their presentation is usually dramatic.

Examples of Famous Fours

Betty Davis, Neil Young, Brian Ferry, Leslie Howard, Daniel Day Lewis, the fictional character Scarlet O'Hara, the fictional character Mary Hartman, Joni Mitchell, Vanessa Redgrave, Gloria Steinem, Edgar Allen Poe, Alan Watts, Cher, Marlon Brando, Michael Jackson, Vincent Van Gogh.

Examples of International Enneagrams

France is an example of an Enneagram number Four personality country. It strives to be unique and different and to not conform to other international standards. The French have an "artistic temperament."

Animals

A mourning dove and a noble black racing horse are examples of Four animals.

Typical Family History

Fours get their special sense of self from their father. They also remember being rejected or emotionally abandoned by the mother. This turns them towards their father. There is a closeness to the father, but it is more of an antagonist or negative energy in that special tie with the father. They often hear their parents messages as "Don't count on my being here for you. Don't be close." This caused the Four child to retreat inward to their emotions and fantasies.

Possible Problems

Fours over-react to criticism. They dislike people who do not take them seriously when they are into their suffering moods. Fours tend to exaggerate or dramatize their life experiences in order to make themselves seem more interesting. They dislike feeling ordinary and will try to set themselves apart from others. Consequently, they often feel isolated and lacking in authenticity. They have difficulty with intimate relationships. Fours can spend time in fantasy instead of action.

When life is going especially bad, Fours can become morbid and have a tendency to attempt to attach themselves to other people. They are then more concerned with what other people think of them and their fear of rejection is increased. At their unhealthiest they can become emotionally blocked and can become self-destructive through drugs or even suicide.

5 Observer

Other Personality Names That Have Been Used for the Type Five Personality
- Sage
- Thinker
- Knower
- Hoarder
- Watcher
- Encyclopedia

Key to the Five Personality
- They overly resist an emptiness that comes from not knowing all the facts about everything in their lives.
- Instead, they fill themselves with many facts and lots of knowledge, trying to understand and get the "big picture."

Self Definition/Self Image
" I am perceptive."

Personality Traits
- Fives are minimalists and aware of the value of things.
- They are independent.
- Fives will not usually rock the boat.
- They are often uneasy at parties and social gatherings and tend to be found in the back of the room.
- Fives view life as a problem to be solved.
- Fives are good at independent work.
- They live in their thoughts and have difficulty expressing feelings.
- Fives are usually private, low profile people and avoid self-disclosure.
- Fives can stand back and view life dispassionately.
- They can easily spend time alone and are self-sufficient.
- Fives like privacy and a place where they can be alone.
- They love acquiring knowledge.
- They tend to be stingy with their knowledge and money, etc.
- Fives are turned off by brash, loud people or events.

Preoccupations
- Concern with privacy.
- Restrict or minimize their personal needs as a way of staying uninvolved.
- Control of unpredictable feelings and reactions.
- Interest in analytical knowledge as a substitute for emotional experience.

Common Occupations
Fives excel in positions requiring logical thinking. They are often employed in the following occupations:
Librarian, research scientist, academic, archaeologist, computer worker, accountant, staff worker, technician, writer.

Method of Communication
Fives tend to say as little as possible. Fives can have a dry, low affect to their voice. They communicate about facts and information in a detached way. They report data without emotional involvement.

Examples of Famous Fives
Chopin, Emily Dickinson, Henry Fonda, Bill Gates, Stephen King, Howard Hughes, Buddha, Thomas Edison, Henry Kissinger, Thomas Edison, Albert Einstein, George Lucas, Bobby Fisher.

Examples of International Enneagrams
Japan is an example of an Enneagram number Five personality country. It is logical, frugal and its people control their feelings and reactions.

Animals
An owl and a fox are examples of Five animals.

Typical Family History
Fives get more of their special sense of themselves from their mother, and get less contact from their father. Fives have one parent that was either physically or emotionally intrusive, so the child closed down its feelings in

order to get away from this oppression. They interpreted their parents messages as "Don't be close. Don't belong."

Possible Problems

Fives become upset with people who are pushy and make demands on them. Fives tend to over accumulate knowledge. They can feel despair and withdraw from others and can become observers of life instead of participants.

When life is going especially bad, Fives have a tendency to plan and day-dream more, while rarely actually following through with the plans. If they become mentally unhealthy, they can become antagonistic towards those who are critical of their dreams or beliefs. They might identify with radical causes or ideas. Fives can become paranoid and frightened by life.

6 Loyalist

Other Personality Names That Have Been Used for the Type Six Personality
- Devil's Advocate
- Groupist
- Loyal Skeptic
- Defender
- Security Type
- Facilitator
- Doubter
- Guardian
- Problem Finder
- Questioner
- Supporter

Key to the Six Personality
- They overly resist separation or rejection from family or a group.
- Instead, they find security by learning to be loyal and to avoid the disapproval of their chosen group. However sometimes they can question or challenge authority for constructive purposes.

Self Definition/Self Image
"I am loyal. I am cautious."

Personality Traits
- They need security and certainty.
- Sixes have a long attention span.
- Sixes can be rebellious, usually in a positive way.
- They are good at planning and implementing strategies.
- They are usually on the alert for danger.
- Sixes are hard working and take their responsibilities seriously.
- Sixes view life as threatening.
- Sixes want to be safe and to overcome fears.
- Sixes can be afraid of being abandoned.

- They like predictability.
- Sixes usually believe in loyalty and duty.
- Sixes have a sense of tradition.
- They can have difficulty making decisions.
- Sixes believe life can be very demanding, and they are very sensitive to dangers.
- They require logical proof of things.
- They may have a nervous energy about them.

Preoccupations
- Alertness to danger.
- Issues with authority – whether to submit or rebel.
- Procrastination can take the place of doing.
- Suspicious of other's motives.
- Scanning the environment looking for clues that explain their inner sense of impending danger.

Common Occupations
Sixes excel in positions that have logical methods for determining the correct course of action. They are often employed in the following occupations:
Instructor at school, engineer, armed forces officers, policeman, fireman, attorney, government jobs, machinist, builder, scientist.

Method of Communication
Sixes often talk about the group they are in. They can argue with you on an analytical level, weighing the pros and cons. They can caution you to take heed of various dangers. Their speech pattern might be halting. Sixes often take big breaths and speak a long time on each breath.

Examples of Famous Sixes
Sigmund Freud, Krishnamurti, Woody Allen, Sonny Bono, the fictional character Hamlet, Steve McQueen, David Letterman, Bob Newhart, George Bush, Newt Gingrich.

Examples of International Enneagrams
Germany is an example of an Enneagram number Six personality country. It is loyal and has safety and security issues.

Animals
A wolf, a loyal German shepherd, and a hare in full flight are examples of Sixes.

Typical Family History
Sixes get their special sense of self from their mother. The Six child tends to be raised with ambiguity in its rules. Unlike One children who have clear rules, Sixes tend to feel as if they were in a mine field of rules and that breaking a rule they didn't even know existed could lead to dire consequences. One wrong step can be disastrous and you never know which step that will be. Parents tend to have inconsistent rules with limits not clearly defined. The Six child heard their parents messages as "Don't do that. Be careful. If you don't watch out, it'll get you."

Possible Problems
Sixes become upset with people who dispute their reality. They also react negatively to people who appear to be feeble-minded.

Sixes tend to run from their fear and seek their security in their family or in groups. They dislike deviations from any group ethics that would threaten the group and hence their security.

When life is going especially poorly Sixes have a tendency to be more anxious about how they appear to others. They can feel more incompetent and seem unable to act on their own. They complain more about their problems. If they become mentally unhealthy, Sixes could become self-destructive, or they might become aggressive towards others.

7 Optimist

Other Personality Names That Have Been Used for the Type Seven Personality
- Visionary
- Planner
- Generalist
- Fun Lover
- Epicurean
- Enjoyer
- Cheerer
- Enthusiast
- Dreamer
- Networker
- Materialist
- Adventurer

Key to the Seven Personality
- They overly resist pain and suffering.
- Instead, they avoid pain by focusing on pleasure, opportunity and planning for the future and focusing on happy things.

Self Definition/Self Image
"I am fun. I see the bright side of life."

Personality Traits
- Sevens can be charming and easy to get along with.
- Sevens are optimists and have dreams and visions of what is possible.
- Sevens are free-spirited and spontaneous.
- Sevens look for the awe and wonder in life.
- They often have discriminating taste in food, clothing and many other areas of life.
- Sevens dislike authority but usually avoid conflicts with authority by removing themselves from the problem.
- They love travel, new adventures and excitement.
- Sevens see life as having endless possibilities.

- They have knowledge about many subjects and can "wear many hats."
- Sevens love to celebrate life.
- Sevens pursue stimulation and peak experiences.
- They often have lots of new ideas.
- Sevens usually are lively and talkative.
- Sevens tend to work in spurts.

Preoccupations
- Maintaining a high level of stimulation and activities in order to stay feeling "high."
- Pleasant talking, planning and intellectualizing.
- Diffusing negative feelings by maintaining a smoke screen of activity.
- Using charm as the first line of defense against fear.

Common Occupations
Sevens excel in planning or researching new concepts. They are better in staff positions than line positions. They are often employed in the following occupations:
Consultant, management staff, sales, public relations, storyteller, comedian, entrepreneur, writer, scientist.

Method of Communication
Sevens are good conversationalists. They usually conduct friendly, agreeable discussions about ideas. They are good story tellers, and can get you involved in their personal stories. Sevens tend not to talk about feelings. Instead they talk about plans and theories on an intellectual and abstract level.

Examples of Famous Sevens
Carl Sagan, Henry David Thoreau, Kurt Vonnegut, Jack Nicholson, Professor Hal Cohen, Bill Cosby, Ram Dass, Loni Anderson, Steve Allen, Chevy Chase, Joseph Campbell, Alan King, Dick Van Dyke, Jonathan Winters, Tom Hanks, Robin Williams.

Examples of International Enneagrams
Ireland is an example of an Enneagram number Seven personality country. It looks at the bright side of life and even

celebrates after funerals. Brazil is another example of a Seven country with their carnivals and their attitude of celebration.

Animals

A monkey is an example of a number Seven.

Typical Family History

Sevens get their special sense of self from their mother. They were probably mother's special person and during some early point in their life this special connection was lost. The perceived loss left a deep fear. Still the Seven remembers their childhood as pleasant and was out of touch with the fear and pain that might have occurred while they were growing up. The Seven is left with the feeling that it can't quite trust life and wants a backup or a "plan B."

Possible Problems

Sevens are upset by people who try to force or manipulate them to do things which are not fun.

Sevens tend to make many plans but actually carry out few of these plans. They dream rather than do the work necessary for their plans to reach completion.

When life is going especially bad, Sevens have a tendency to be resentful of what life is dealing them. They cease their usual optimism and find fault with things. They might become rude and aggressive. They may try to forget their anxieties by addictions to food, sex, alcohol, drugs, etc. When giving up one vice or bad habit, they tend to indulge in another.

8 Champion

Other Personality Names That Have Been Used for the Type Eight Personality
- Boss
- Leader
- Dominator
- Challenger
- Confronter
- Chief
- Controller
- Thrill seeker
- Statesman
- Asserter
- Questioner

Key to the Eight Personality
- They overly resist weakness within themselves.
- Instead, they become powerful and stand up against others.

Self Definition/Self Image
"I can do it. I am powerful."

Personality Traits
- Eights let people know where they stand with them.
- They can be defenders of the underdog and the weak.
- Eights are assertive and want the world to notice them.
- They can be really good friends.
- Eights view life in terms of winning and losing.
- They often have a high sense of integrity.
- Eights work hard and know how to get things done.
- They want to be self-reliant.
- Eights generally are powerful, strong, self-confident people, and will fight for what is right.
- They are direct and straight forward.
- For Eights, decision making is easy.
- They live life intensely.

Preoccupations
- Control of personal objects, space and people.
- Excessive life; "too much, too loud, too late, etc."
- Denial of other's points of view in favor of a single legitimate opinion that supports the Eight's security.

Common Occupations
Eights excel in positions where they have a lot of power. They are often employed in the following occupations: *Armed forces sergeant or officer, police officer, attorney, sports athlete, union organizer, business manager.*

Method of Communication
Eights are usually very direct in what they say and in the way they say it. They can use imperatives and might have an earthy language, but not necessarily. They can sound arrogant and can complain about people who don't come up to their standards.

Examples of Famous Eights
Beethoven, General George Patton, Fritz Pearls, Henry the Eighth, Mr. T, Joan Rivers, Pablo Picasso, Bette Midler, Danny DeVito, Nietzsche, Rhea Perlman, Charles Bronson, Jesse Jackson, President Lyndon B. Johnson, Rush Limbaugh, Lee Marvin, George C. Scott.

Examples of International Enneagrams
Spain is an example of an Enneagram number Eight personality country. It is macho and rejects weakness.

Animals
A rhinoceros, tiger, and bull are examples of Eights.

Typical Family History
Eights usually get their special sense of self from their mother. They tend to interpret the events of their childhood as feeling dominated by bigger, stronger people who wanted to control them. This may be either a physical or an emotional domination. The Eight child challenged this

domination even though it had to fight against adults or older children representing overwhelming odds. They interpreted their early messages as "Don't be you. Don't feel what you feel."

Possible Problems

Eights are upset by weak people who won't stand up for themselves. Eights will tend to be champions of justice, law, and order; Eights can fight to uphold these concepts. They deny they have any weaknesses and can scare others with their tough exterior.

When life is going especially bad, Eights have a tendency to withdraw and to become introverted. They become stingy with their money, time and help for others. They might cheat or lie to others. If they become mentally unhealthy Eights can become paranoid and dangerous, possibly getting into physical fights.

9 Peacemaker

Other Personality Names That Have Been Used for the Type Nine Personality
- Mediator
- Negotiator
- Easygoer
- Acceptor
- Preservationist

Key to the Nine Personality
- They overly resist conflict and strife.
- Instead, they go with the flow and seek harmony and peace at almost any price.

Self Definition/Self Image
"I am easy going."

Personality Traits
- Nines are good at seeing all sides of an issue.
- Nines tend not to sweat the small stuff.
- Nines have big hearts.
- They can be there for others and don't expect anything in return.
- Nines tend to put things off until almost the last minute.
- Nines are "laid back" easy-going people.
- They prefer to work at their own pace.
- Nines are balanced and "go with the flow."
- They usually are good listeners and diplomatic.
- Nines are accepting and passive.
- They can numb themselves.
- Nines are good at avoiding pressure.
- Nines enjoy hanging out with their friends.
- They like to stay comfortable and undisturbed.

Preoccupations
- Conflict between positive belief and doubts often producing indecisiveness.
- Difficulty saying "no."

Chapter 1 The Enneagram 49

- They often adhere to the desires of others as a means of finding security.

Common Occupations

Nines excel where they can perform routine work or within a lot of structure or where they can bring peace between conflicting people. They are often employed in the following occupations:
Detail work in a manufacturing plant, arbitrator, diplomat, ambassador, administrator, public relations, bureaucrat.

Method of Communication

Nines can tell long epic stories with far too many details. They also like to listen and to hear what is happening with others. They tend to complain, not like a One or an Eight but like a resigned complaining. They are usually not upset, but they can sound a little depressed. They can have a monotone voice. The last sound in a sentence can drop down in pitch.

Examples of Famous Nines

Hubert Humphrey, Julia Child, Gerald Ford, Dwight Eisenhower, Jean Stapleton, Alfred Hitchcock, Peter Falk, Dean Martin, Abraham Lincoln.

Examples of International Enneagrams

Barbados is an example of an Enneagram number Nine personality country. It's people are patient, easy going and laid back.

Animals

Donkeys, elephants and sloths are examples of Nines.

Typical Family History

Nines can get their special sense of self from either their mother and/or their father. Generally, they are not as criticized or controlled as the One child but are victims of benign neglect. Nine children tend to perceive themselves as overlooked and not loved enough or listened to by their parents. Typically, the Nine child's show of anger did not produce its desired results. Consequently they formed the habit of discounting their own essential needs. They interpreted their parent's messages as "Don't bother me. Don't exist. Go away."

Possible Problems

Nines are upset by people who cause conflict or confront them. Nines tend to seek harmony at any cost. They can even ignore parts of reality in order to deny any knowledge of conflict. This can often result in laziness, possibly sitting in front of the television and getting fat.

When life is going especially bad, Nines experience self-doubt, and have more difficulty making decisions. They can be resistant to change and withdraw from life. They may have a tendency to despair and think life is too demanding and dangerous.

Growth

Growth for each personality comes when we realize in our own life how we express our Enneagram type. Then it becomes possible to move beyond the constraints of our particular Enneagram number.

Each of the nine Enneagram personality types sees the world in their individual distortion. To correct this distortion, individual prescriptions are needed to accurately perceive reality.

The exaggerated traits of each personality do have many useful, positive features. These traits were very useful in building our individual egos. It is not necessary to undo or eliminate these personality traits. It is the exaggerated negative constraints that now, as adults, limit us in our desire to become free and whole.

For example a 1995 study by two psychologists (J. Clayton Lafferty and Lorrain Colletti) found that Perfectionists (Enneagram type One) were 75 percent more likely to have headaches and gastrointestinal and cardiovascular problems. This was a 10 year study of 9,211 managers and professional people. Of course the different Enneagram personality types can be expected to have different physical problems.

We can learn to let go of the unhealthy aspects of personality while allowing our basic personalities to remain. Simply being aware of the truth of our personality allows us to more clearly see why we behave as we do.

Growth for Ones

Ones tend to fear that their closely controlled cold anger will rage out of control. They fear that being wrong and at fault will make them angry. They must face this fear and move through it before major growth can happen.

For Ones Personal Growth Can Occur When They Are:
- More into the enjoyment of life and less concerned with everything being perfect.
- More aware of the correctness of different peoples' values and less critical of others.
- More relaxed and less stern.
- More aware of their own goodness and less critical of themselves.
- More playful and less serious.
- More truthful and more willing to express feelings.
- More aware that the world is perfect just as it is, and less apt to try to change the world.
- More accepting to go "one step at a time" and less impatient with life.
- More actual accepting of things as they are and less pretentious about being happy while being internally angry.

Ones should keep in mind that what they perceive as demands from others are really the demands of their own internal judge. They would do well to remember that the world is progressing just as it is. The world will never be perfect, nor indeed is it desirable for it to be perfect. Life is not perfect, but is a process of growing, day by day. Living need not be solemn and serious, but can in fact can be relaxing and fun.

Life task
To achieve a sense of serenity with a body secure in its capacities. As projections are worked through and resentment has been tamed, compassion becomes possible.

Meditation
I let go of judgments and resentments and accept life just as it is.

Growth for Twos

Twos tend to panic over what would happen to them if they no longer solely focused on helping others. They fear that they would lose their identity. They must face this fear and move through it before major growth can happen.

For Twos Personal Growth Can Occur When They Are:

- More giving of unconditional, spiritual love and less manipulative helping other people while expecting something in return.
- Generating more self-esteem from within and less from others.
- Living a simple, less complicated life.
- More acknowledging of their own needs, and less concerned with the needs of others.
- More self-accepting and less self-depreciating.
- More aware of flattery as a method of control and less manipulative of others using flattery.
- More giving of support with no strings attached and less approval seeking.

Twos should recognize their hidden needs and feelings, especially their negative feelings. They should remember that they do matter, that they are important in themselves and not because of their service to others.

Life task

To move from dependence upon the approval of other's to knowledge of one's own personal strength to meet one's own needs. Often this understanding comes through personal loss. The resulting depression can often lead to a more acute self-assessment and the understanding of their work to be done.

Meditation

I am lovable and loved just as I am.

Growth for Threes

Threes fear the appearance of failure and tend to stretch the truth in order to present themselves as successful. They can grow when they take time from their whirlwind of activities to stop and look at the deceptions they have created in their lives.

For Threes Personal Growth Can Occur When They Are:

- More trusting of the world to operate efficiently on its own and less concerned with being in control.
- More cooperative and less competitive.
- More truthful and less boasting about themselves.
- More cooperative and less vain and concerned about status.
- More self-assured and less afraid of failure.
- More authentic and less influenced by others.
- More focused on enduring values of character and integrity and less of the superficial belief that "if it works, it is truth."
- More interested in self-improvement and meditation practices, and less afraid of dealing with shortcomings.
- More cooperative with others and less seeking attention or praise.
- More satisfied in the present moment and less replacing of personal happiness with long working hours.

Threes can go beyond the fear of failure by committing themselves to a group or cause they believe is of greater importance than themselves. They can realize that they can't do everything alone, and in fact, others can do some things better. They can remember that the end does not justify the means.

Life task

Threes have to struggle to stop valuing themselves only in terms of their performance and the results they produce in life. Learning to stop, reflect, feel and to question what they are doing can bring redemption.

Meditation
I am competent and worthwhile exactly as I am.

Growth for Fours

Fours fear the commonplace and ordinary and tend to be dissatisfied with life. They feel that reality is boring and they will become lost in a humdrum existence. They must face this fear and become more contented with things the way they are before major growth can occur.

For Fours Personal Growth Can Occur When They Are:

- More creative and less overly emotional.
- More aware of the oneness of all life and less self-pitying and envious of others.
- Less procrastinating and more action-oriented.
- More diligent and hard-working and less self sabotaging.
- More instinctive and less concerned with feelings.
- More accepting of the way things are and less longing to be special.
- More assertive and feeling less like a victim.
- More honest about one's true Self and less thinking of oneself as a special person.

Fours can learn to not take everything so personally and can discipline themselves to accomplish tasks regardless of their ever changing moods. They can recognize that they are part of humanity and that they are not unique and different. They can learn to remember that happiness consists of accepting what cannot be changed, and not struggle with wanting things to be different.

Life task

To achieve a sense of reality of the here and now, in the present moment, and to be able to muster the strength of commitment, balance and harmony in accepting all that is. Uncovering grief and sadness in its origins can allow an experience of life without displacement. To extend awareness out of self absorption into the ordinary events of life. To resist the tendency to be withdrawn and uncommitted in emotional relationships because of fears of disappointment and abandonment and rejection. When this sense of loss and deprivation is resolved, fours can see life differently and allow themselves to be happy. To struggle against the tendency of being envious of others. To overcome the longing for what was or could have been and be in the present moment, which is the only place where healing and transformation can take place.

Meditation
My life is in the present moment and I am satisfied with reality as it is now.

Growth for Fives

Fives tend to fear what would happen to them if they didn't understand life. They can fear getting immersed in the stuff of life without having detached insights about the underling meanings. They must face this fear and move through it before major growth can occur.

For Fives Personal Growth Can Occur When They Are:

- More willing to share with others and become less stingy.
- More involved in real living and less in observing life.
- More assertive and less afraid of the use of power.
- More relaxed and less intense.
- More of a "We can do it" attitude, cooperating with others, and less often a loner.
- More willing to share knowledge with others and less grasping for knowledge.
- More compassionate with others and less judgmental of emotional, feeling people.
- More original in their thinking and less filing and cataloging of learned facts or data.
- More willing to be openly known as an active player in life and less of a minimal participant in life.

Fives can replace insecure thoughts with confidence that comes from believing they are in fact knowledgeable enough to live bravely in reality with the rest of humanity.

Life task

To gain knowledge of life by moving into action instead of being an outside observer. To struggle against camouflaging their existence and reducing their needs to a minimum so as to call as little attention as possible to themselves. To move out of the dominance of their minds (where they remain aloof) and to move towards people and life. To pursue their interests without isolating themselves from others.

Meditation
Everyone is an equal reservoir of the same life energy that is alive within me.

Growth for Sixes

Sixes tend to fear what would happen if their group or friends reject or disapprove of them. They must face this fear and move through it before major growth can occur.

For Sixes Personal Growth Can Occur When They Are:
- Trusting themselves more and paying less attention to self-doubt.
- More self-assured and less anxious.
- More trusting of others and less defensive.
- More allowing of feeling and intuiting and less talking or thinking.
- More trusting of others and the universe and less concerned about security.
- More self-affirming and less worried about what society thinks.
- More comfortable with life and less cynical.
- More aware of the shades of gray and less thinking in terms of black and white.
- More responsible and less indecisive.
- More faithful towards the positive progress of life and less self-doubting.

Sixes can overcome their fear of being different from other members of their group and become more independent. They need the courage to risk doing new things instead of doing the same old things repeatedly.

Life task
To achieve the spiritual faith that nothing from outside can hurt their essence. To attain trust and strength from their courage. To become their own authority. To realize that there is enough love around to protect them. To regain their personal freedom by realizing that they don't have to depend on an outside authority. To regain their sense of confidence in their own abilities and act on their own behalf.

Meditation
I am filled with strength and decisiveness.

Growth for Sevens

Sevens tend to fear pain and suffering. They fantasize new plans and stay busy leading the "good life" to distract themselves from any frightening, painful thoughts. They must face this fear and move through it before major growth can occur.

For Sevens Personal Growth Can Occur When They Are:

- More focused on sobriety and being aware in the moment and less in pursuit of pleasure.
- More engaged in actual work and production and less planning.
- More concerned with quality and less with gluttony.
- More aware of life as a mix of both joy and pain and less seeing life as just pleasure.
- More giving to others and less grasping.
- More willing to experience unhappiness and less preoccupied with being happy at any cost.
- More willing to just observe and know and less dependent on being with others.
- More satisfied with life as it is and less feeling deprived of life's joys.
- More willing to wait and work for things and less impulsive.

Sevens should stop running away from painful reality and realize that life contains both pain and pleasure. They should be willing to complete their plans even if that is difficult and painful. They should trust life to be O.K. as it is and not always try to escape life by looking for sweetness and pleasure.

Life task

To work with a sense of proportion and balance, anchored in the present moment. Dealing with, and not always avoiding pain can serve as a steadying point of focus. To sit quietly with themselves knowing that they no longer have to run away from life. To have open total commitment to people and projects. To struggle against planning another "pleasant option" when things get difficult or boring. To accept all aspects of life and not just those that are peak experiences.

Meditation
I can connect with others emotionally and am open to both the pain and joy of relationships.

Growth for Eights

Eights tend to fear personal weakness and control by others. They fear that revealing what causes them anxiety or pain will allow others to take advantage of them. They must face this fear and move through it before major growth can happen.

For Eights Personal Growth Can Occur When They Are:
- More aware of life in shades of gray and less judgmental and see life less as black or white.
- More accepting of life as it is. Less trying to make life fair and just.
- More tender and vulnerable. Less macho and tough.
- More powerful and self-restrained in the use of power and less abusive.
- More caring for others and less self-centered.
- More liked and less feared by other people.
- More concerned with family and friends and less concerned with money.
- More of a leader of others and more helpful towards others, and less aggressive.
- More willing to see other peoples' point of view and less obsessed with being right.

Eights can learn to remember not to use their power to control others, but instead realize that others have rights. They can guide others and work in a true spirit of cooperation, openness and love. Eights can learn to be willing to drop or soften their hard outer shell.

Life task
To realize the truth and justice in each moment's flow of reality. To accept personal weakness and not demand control of all aspects of life.

Meditation
I will use my strength to promote growth and love instead of intimidation and attack.

Growth for Nines

Nines tend to fear conflict and strong emotions, so they minimize and deny even the very existence of their emotions. They fear that emotional discord will destroy their own personal control. They must face this fear and move through it before major growth can happen.

For Nines Personal Growth Can Occur When They Are:
- More active in the pursuit of life and less withdrawn from life.
- More successful in business and life and less problems setting deadlines and timetables.
- More action oriented and less oriented towards procrastination.
- More of a self-starter and less dependent on direction from others.
- More aware of God's total love for them and less for love from others.
- More supportive of friends, but less dependent on others.
- More aware of what is happening and less daydreaming and escaping.
- More fixed on the present reality and less concerned with eventual goals.
- More engaged in physical exercise and less lazy.

Nines can learn to be more flexible and accept change. They can increase their flexibility by learning new ways of expressing their feelings even if this upsets others. They can also work to increase their natural abilities, giving more value to their own self-worth.

Life task
To experience love which is guided by the strength of their taking appropriate actions in any given situation, including conflict.

Meditation
My life has great value and I possess high self-esteem.

CHAPTER 2

ADDITIONAL ENNEAGRAM INFORMATION

> *"Irrespective of our conscious convictions, each one of us, without exception, being a particle of the general mass, is somewhere attached to, colored by, or even undermined by the Spirit which goes through the mass. Freedom stretches only as far as the limits of our consciousness."*
> — *Carl Jung*

Chapter 2 Additional Enneagram information

Overview of Chapter

This chapter is included for those who are interested in more details of the Enneagram. Most readers will have gotten the personal usefulness of the Enneagram from the preceding chapter and can skip this chapter and go on to chapter three.

Although there is much disagreement among teachers concerning the history of the Enneagram of Personality Types, there is no disagreement over the value of its study.

This chapter will quickly touch on the history of the symbol of the Enneagram and how this symbol was introduced to the West.

We will also explain some of the theory of how the Enneagram symbol works and how it became created into a system of knowledge about the functioning of personality types.

As we continue through this chapter we come to understand that although we have one "core" type which constitutes our personality, there are four more points on the Enneagram which make up the total map of how our personality functions. This concept is explained in the section on "Movement along the lines" and shows the reader how to verify one's "core" type.

One common question concerns the similarity and differences of the Enneagram of Personality Types and the Myers Briggs Personality Profile. Although both describe personalities, the Myers Briggs looks at an individual's behavior while the Enneagram looks at the motivation that underlie the behavior. This is a significant difference since two individuals can exhibit the same performance while having completely opposite inner motivation.

Additionally the Enneagram is more spiritual and group based, showing the interrelationships of various personalities, while the Myers Briggs is more individual based. Finally, most people find the Enneagram is easier to learn and provides more feedback on their core issues and growth potential.

History of the Enneagram

The word Enneagram comes from the Greek, *ennea*, which means nine and *grammos* which means point. Together they mean nine points. Enneagram is pronounced "any-a-gram."

There is much disagreement as to exactly when or where the Enneagram originated but it is generally thought to have its roots in the Middle East around two thousand years ago. The geometric form of the nine pointed star in a circle was recorded during that time period.

About nine hundred years ago, a mystic sect called the Sufis (especially the Bektashi Order) is known to have included the Enneagram in their spiritual practices.

Around 1925 an unusual Russian mystic named George Gurdjieff began teaching the Enneagram to his students at his "Institute for the Harmonious Development of Man" located in Paris. Gurdjieff said that he learned of the Enneagram in his travels to the Middle East. The Enneagram was used to describe movement and change in various processes – not just personalities.

Later Oscar Ichazo also taught the Enneagram of Personality Types in Chile and Bolivia. He is said to have more fully developed the descriptions of each of the nine personalities and their position on the Enneagram. Most of the people who learned the Enneagram trace their teachings back to the work of Oscar Ichazo.

A psychiatrist named Claudio Naranjo added western psychiatric understanding to the growing body of Enneagram knowledge. He helped develop a very accessible psychological model that most people can easily understand.

The Enneagram of Personality Types has spread very rapidly in the last ten years, and at the end of 1995 many hundreds of thousands of people have taken seminars on the Enneagram. Also more than one million books were printed on various aspects of the Enneagram.

Today various church groups, universities, business consultants, educators, and psychologists find the

Chapter 2 Additional Enneagram information

Enneagram a valuable key to understanding themselves and their relationship to God.

In August of 1994 the First International Enneagram Conference was held at Stanford University and more than 1,400 people from 34 countries attended. The conference had an amazing 142 seminar presenters with topics divided into various categories of interest which included:
- Assessment/Research/History Track
- Business Track
- Education Track
- Experiential Practices Track
- Spiritual Track
- Therapy/Medicine Track

Enneagram Theory

The Enneagram of Personality Types began as an Oral Tradition and different teachers each have their individual views of the theory and use of the Enneagram. Naturally there is some disagreement over various aspects of the Enneagram theory.

According to Enneagram theory, each of us belongs to one of nine distinct personality types. By way of heredity, family life and the cultural environment, we developed a personality, and our own way of dealing with the world. Our real Self then became masked by the personality we chose as a mechanism to cope with life, as a child. Now, as adults, our actions are still influenced by these childhood habits of relating to the world.

The Three Groups

The Enneagram of Personality Types probably grew from the discovery that there are three things that occupy humans. The first is **feeling** some emotion such as sad, glad guilt etc. The second is **doing** something, like walking scratching etc. The third is **thinking**, such as planning some activity for tomorrow.

Each individual is occupied with one of these activities more than the other two. Therefore humanity can be divided into three groups: the **feeling or relationship** group, the **doing or anger** group and the **thinking or fear** group.

Relationship group (2, 3, 4)

The relationship group is also known as the **heart or feeling group** since they are seen as more emotional and somewhat more concerned with feelings than the other two groups. The other groups, under the surface, are just as emotional. However, it is the relationship group that displays their emotions more publicly. The relationship group has concerns with the way they look and the image that they project. This group could dress in a variety of ways anywhere from a successful executive to a hippie artist. The thing they all have in common is they operate primarily from their feelings.

Anger group (8, 9, 1)

The anger group is also known as the **doing, gut or instinctive group** since they operate more from their gut instincts and intuitions. They are more spontaneous in their reactions than the calculating, fear group. The anger group has various anger issues. They may either have cold anger, a hot anger or a denial of anger.

Fear group (5, 6, 7)

The fear group is also known as the **head or intellectual group** since they are more thinking oriented than the other groups. The fear group has concerns about coping with the world. They use logic to try to make sense of reality. The fear group is seen as more objective and impersonal in their thoughts than the other groups. By contrast, the relationship group's thoughts are more about their feelings about personal relationships.

Triangle Symbol

These three groups are connected by a triangle creating the basic core of the Enneagram symbol as shown below. The three points of the triangle signify the three groups. The circle around the triangle is symbolic of the unity of all humanity.

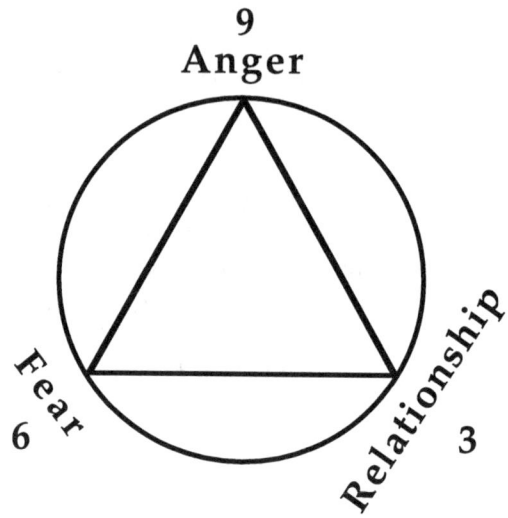

The Nine Numbers

These three groups are further subdivided again by three resulting in nine personality numbers or types.

The Enneagram Symbol with the Three Groups

On the following page is the Enneagram symbol. It is helpful to visually understand how the Enneagram symbol relates to the three groups and also to the nine Enneagram numbers. This figure shows that the two, three and four are the subdivisions of the relationship or heart group. Similarly the five, six and seven are subdivisions of the fear or head group. The eight, nine and one are subdivisions of the anger or gut group.

This is the time to verify that your Enneagram number does coincide with the group that you believe you are in. If not look at the section "Movement Along the Lines" and also the section "Dominant Wing."

Chapter 2 Additional Enneagram information 75

The Enneagram Symbol

To symbolize the nine Enneagram numbers, the Ancient Masters chose a circle connecting a nine-pointed star. Each point on the star depicts one of the nine personality types. The two lines connecting each number indicate relationships between them. Notice the triangle from the three groups inside the Enneagram symbol. The triangle connects the numbers Three, Six and Nine, which are the center and core points of the three groups.

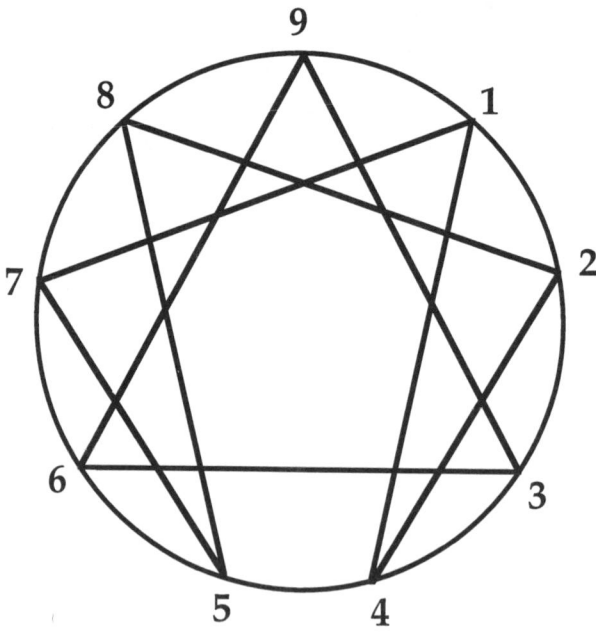

Movement Along the Lines

The Enneagram symbol connects each number with two other numbers by way of straight lines as shown in the Enneagram diagram on the next page. The direction of the arrow indicates the stress point. For example, the stress point of number One would be Four. So when a One is under stress, they tend to operate from the personality of the Four and may suffer and feel misunderstood by others. It is stressful to be in the stress point, so the One will not like to suffer and is more comfortable just being angry instead of actually suffering like the Four. If the One comes to terms with these issues of the stress point, growth occurs.

Conversely, the direction against the arrow indicates the security point. The security point of number One would be Seven. Therefore, when a One is feeling secure they tend to operate from the personality of the Seven where the right and wrong judgmental thinking diminishes. They might be more playful, and less a perfectionist. Healing can happen at the security point. This is going to the very foundation of personality. When the One comes to terms with the issues of the security point, then healing can occur. However, the security point is not always a comfortable place to be. The One will not really trust the Seven personality because it is not serious and perfect enough.

The direction of movement of the arrows on the triangle is counter clockwise. Starting at one we have the numbers 142857. Interestingly, the direction of movement of the arrows on the star is the same as for the decimal equivalent of the fraction $1/7$ which equals the decimal .142857142857142857 ad infinitum. This is a recurring decimal and has no end.

It is useful to look at the security and stress points to verify our Enneagram personality type and to better understand how our personality changes as we move along the lines of the Enneagram symbol.

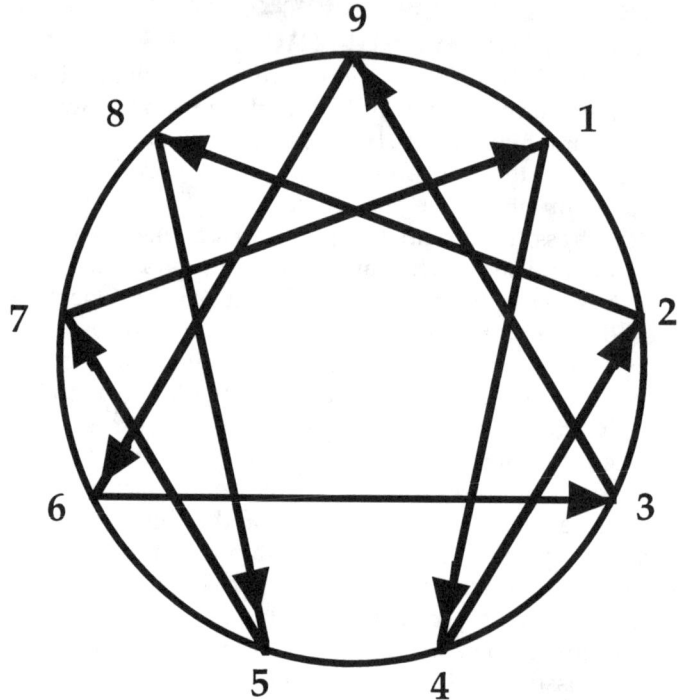

The stress and security points of the nine personality numbers are as follows:

1. The **One's** stress point is Four so under stress, they tend to suffer and feel misunderstood by others. The security point of number One would be Seven, so here they might be more playful, and less a perfectionist.

2. The **Two's** stress point is Eight, so here the Two is more likely to get angry. The Two's security point is Four, so here the Two is more likely to dramaticize feelings.

3. The **Three's** stress point is Nine, so here the Three is more likely to be out of touch with feelings and to operate more mechanically. The Three's security point is Six, so here the Three is more cooperative and aware of the group and less concerned about status.

4. The **Four's** stress point is Two, so here the Four is more likely to please, charm and flatter others. The Four's security point is One, so here the Four is more likely to be neater and more of a perfectionist.

5. The **Five's** stress point is Seven, so here the Five is more likely to plan and day-dream instead of taking action. The Five's security point is Eight, so here the Five is more able to be assertive and involved with others in life.

6. The **Six's** stress point is Three, so here the Six is likely to become anxious and to take action defensively. The Six's security point is Nine, so here the Six is more able to relax, make decisions and be more self-assured.

7. The **Seven's** stress point is One, so here the Seven is likely to be judgmental, pessimistic and perfectionistic. The Seven's security point is Five, so here the Seven will move into work and production, and spend less time day-dreaming.

8. The **Eight's** stress point is Five, so here the Eight is more likely to run away and hide. The Eight's security point is Two, so here the Eight is more able to play, be joyful, get silly and please people.

9. The **Nine's** stress point is Six, so here the Nine is more likely to become afraid, self-doubting and indecisive. The Nine's security point is Three, so here the Nine is more energetic, more involved in life, and more successful.

Dominant Wing

Each personality number has two wings. These are the numbers on either side of their core number. These wings account for variations in the core number. In the following chart, personality number One has Nine and Two as wings. Some Enneagram teachers have different views about the wings.

Core Number	The Two Wings
1	9 and 2
2	1 and 3
3	2 and 4
4	3 and 5
5	4 and 6
6	5 and 7
7	6 and 8
8	7 and 9
9	8 and 1

Most people have one dominant wing, and it is useful to discover which wing this is. This wing further defines your individual personality.

People have both wings available to them and they may want to explore how the non-dominant wing functions. This assists in personal growth since if someone has one weak wing, it can significantly cut them off from their potential. You should feel free to explore and use all the positive traits from both your wings.

1. Ones that lean towards the Nine wing tend to be less self concerned, less vain, more easy going, but smile less readily. Ones that lean towards the Two are more concerned with how they look, and more concerned with getting attention from others. They are more dramatic in their presentation, more sensitive to others and more proud.

2. Twos that lean towards the One are lazier and have less energy. They are more concerned with things being right. Twos that lean towards the Three have a harder edge and are more aggressive, but this can be a seductive aggression.

3. Threes that lean towards the Two wing will tend to take on the feelings of others while the Threes that lean toward the Four wing will tend to dramatize their own feelings.

4. Fours that lean towards the Three are more aggressive. They are out in the world getting things accomplished but tend to sabotage success in their personal lives. Fours that lean towards the Five wing are more withdrawn and isolated.

5. Fives that lean towards the Four are more into their feelings, more artistic and more melancholic. Fives that lean towards the Six operate more out of their head and are more likely to be disconnected from their feelings. They can be less emotionally connected with people.

6. Sixes that lean towards the Five are softer, quieter and withdrawn. Sixes that lean towards the Seven are more aggressive, more interactive, and more optimistic.

7. Sevens that lean towards the Six are more unsure of themselves and have a subtle nervous energy. They are more hesitant in their action. Sevens that lean towards the Eight have more of a sense of their own power. They are tougher and more aggressive.

8. Eights that lean towards the Seven operate more from their heads, are more into plans, more intellectual and more idealistic. Eights that lean towards the Nine are more pragmatic and operate more from their gut than from their head.

9. Nines that lean towards the Eight will dress sloppier. They can be more overtly angry. Nines that lean towards the One are more in control of themselves and their environment. They have more of a sense of how things should be. Their anger is more repressed.

Using the Enneagram to Understand Others

Learning your own personality number is only the first part of this test. An even more intriguing part of the Enneagram is using it to understand others. In many ways, this part is more entertaining since most of us can be much less serious when we are examining the personalities of others. We can also get a better understanding of the Enneagram since we often see things in others that we are unable to see in ourselves.

Very often we misread others. We tend to think that everyone reacts the same way we do. But this is not accurate. People react in various ways depending on their primary bias or fixation towards life.

The next several sections were designed to assist you in understanding the personalities of others. This is not always easy, especially for a beginner in the study of the Enneagram. There will probably be people, even in your immediate family, whose Enneagram personality number you mis-type or have difficulty determining.

Physical Characteristics

Sometimes visual clues can help you in determining someone's Enneagram number. The following list of characteristics should not be taken too seriously. There are some people who have none of these characteristics.

Those characteristics of type give an added flavor to the personality numbers. They can often be quite useful in determining someone's personality. The descriptions are for Americans; different countries will have slightly different images or flavors.

1. Ones are not overly concerned with their image but they usually have a proper, neat and well scrubbed look. They might wear color coordinated clothes. Their finger nails are usually clean and trim, but some may bite them. Their hair may not be the latest style but it will usually be clean and neat. Ones often have self-composed faces and bright eyes. They often have an erect spine. There could be a tight quality around the mouth and jaw; this may be associated with thin lips. Because of the rigid way they hold their jaw, there could be a strained quality in their voice. An example of this would be the television journalist Barbara Walters, or the actress Katherine Hepburn. They are usually thin and seldom overweight.

2. Twos usually have a warm and attractive smile. They can have a problem with being overweight (but they could also be thin). They dress to please others, sometimes seductively, but not flashy. They generally wear comfortable clothes that are of a good quality but they may not always be the latest fashion. Twos usually pay close attention when you talk to them.

3. Threes can often look much younger then they are. They often have an "all-American" look (in America). Confident brightness emanates from them. They can have a great smile, but it is cooler and not as warm as the Two's smile. Threes can hold a smile without wavering. Threes dress well; they dress for success and look sharp. They often wear fashionable jewelry and generally wear the appropriate clothes for the occasion. They are usually not overweight although they may have to work at keeping the weight off.

4. Fours often have a sad look, especially in their eyes. Their moist sad eyes may droop at the outer corners. They may dress anywhere from counter culture to the cutting edge of fashion. Fours enjoy different looks and seem to make each outfit work. They might have a one color outfit set off by a scarf or perhaps a belt sash or a colorful beret. Their presentation is usually dramatic. They might use a short dramatic pause before talking. Female Fours often wear jewelry, sometimes rather large.

5. Fives often have an inner sparkle to their eyes. The males may have a beard. Fives are not worried about how they look or about fashion. Unlike the Two, Three, or Four, the Five may wear the same clothes for a few days in a row, however; they will change as soon as they become dirty. Fives do not have open and comfortable smiles. They might have a weak chin.

6. Sixes sometimes have a protruding chin. They usually dress comfortably, rather than stylish, however, they can wear power clothes when needed. They may have a nervous energy about them. They can have a "locked on" type of eye contact that never wavers. Their speech pattern might be halting instead of being a clear and smooth presentation without stops.

7. Sevens can smile a lot. This is not so much the radiant confident smile of a Three nor the warm smile of the Two. It is a strong smile but it may have a nervous quality. Sevens dress fairly well, especially the females. They may have a sense of style, and can be an Epicurean about clothes as well as about food. They might wear a scarf etc., but are not nearly as likely to as Fours. They can be teddy-bearish, but they usually are not fat.

8. Eights can be husky people possibly from body-building or just over-eating. Usually they are not overly concerned about looks, but they can wear massive jewelry. Male Eights might wear an open shirt with a heavy gold chain. They can have an overbearing look, or perhaps an angry glare or obstinate look.

9. Nines can carry too much weight for their frame, but some are thin. They can have somewhat of a heavy energy, as if life were too demanding. They usually dress comfortably and may have well-worn clothes. They may wear jogging suits or other comfortable clothes. At times they may try to dress a little differently. They can look slightly disheveled and might have a messy home. They usually have a fairly relaxed look and an inert quality about them. They are usually fairly pleasant.

Numbers That Could Look Similar

There are a few combinations of personality types that can be particularly difficult to distinguish between.

- **Numbers One and Five** can be confused. The differences are that the Five is more involved in internal control where the One is more involved in outer control – controlling other people and having things "right." Fives look more within themselves while Ones look more outside at others.
- **Numbers One and Six** can be confused. The differences are that the Six is more involved in keeping safe, while the One is more involved in making things right. Both will have many rules, but the Six will have rules about being safe, while the One will have rules about making things right. The counter phobic Six is more likely to be rebellious. The Ones are more likely to be neat and tidy.
- **Numbers Two and Nine** can be confused. The difference is that the Two has more pride features. Twos more often expect to get something in return for what they give. Twos try harder to be pleasing to others. The Nines are more amiable and friendly, but they also have more of a "what you see is what you get" attitude.
- **Numbers Three and Seven** can be confused. The differences are that the Threes don't like to spend much time in thought and are more inclined towards action and producing results. The Seven will be more concerned with keeping their mind stimulated while the Threes will be more concerned with success and status symbols.
- **Numbers Three and Eight** can be confused. The differences are that the Eights are brassier and less concerned with how others see them. The Threes, by contrast, are more concerned with image. The Threes have a smoother and more charming style while the Eights are more confrontive.
- **Numbers Four and Seven** can be confused. The differences are that the Four is more inclined to be

emotional while the Seven is more theoretical and logical. The Four is more overtly sad with more personal problems.

CHAPTER 3
THE GREAT RELIGIONS

> "Our real journey in life is interior; it is a matter of growth, deepening, and of an ever greater surrender to the creative action of love and grace in our hearts."
> – Thomas Merton

Chapter 3 The Great Religions

Overview of Chapter

Even when we are in good physical and mental health, satisfied with our work, and enjoying the support of family and friends, we eventually search for something more: a supreme happiness, peacefulness, or sense of security which we feel is attainable, but only glimpse every now and then.

There is an unending reservoir of peace, happiness, joy, and security within each of us. Some of us seem to have an easier time tapping into this reservoir than others. Yet for all of us, it is there. This is the real self, which many people call the soul or Spirit. Each of us must find this higher inner self and create a solid bond with it, in order to fulfill our search for happiness and peace.

As we grow and learn, we become wiser and more knowledgeable. We learn to compensate for our Enneagram personality type. But the soul or Spirit is beyond the Enneagram and beyond knowledge. It is the source of all wisdom. The soul or Spirit remains whole and unchanged, even as we mature, age, suffer, grow, experience the joys and sorrows of life, and change in other ways.

Throughout human history, the nature of the true self or Spirit has been a topic of great importance. Its study has been central to religion, which is based on the connection between the individual spirit and an infinite, all-powerful Spirit, commonly referred to as God. Religion is the structure through which most people seek to discover their true selves, and acknowledge their connection to God.

The purpose of this chapter is to give an overview of the world's religious thought. This chapter reviews the worlds major religions and gives brief descriptions of how they view the process of relating to God. More importantly this chapter quotes examples of the most significant and best holy scriptures used by these religions.

Why a Spiritual Quest?

At times we may wonder about our own consciousness, and its origin, purpose, and uniqueness. As we contemplate the nature of our minds, we may wonder how the mind is able to question itself. These same questions have puzzled philosophers, scientists, and theologians throughout human history.

We may also wonder who we really are. Each of us seems to have a definite sense of identity: we know the difference between ourselves and others; we all have a deep understanding of our meaning when we use the terms "I" and "me." Yet is our self-perception ever identical to others' perceptions of us? How is our understanding of ourselves influenced by our culture or other external forces? The mystery of who we are, of which self-concept is the most accurate, is an extremely important but complex question.

Our minds perceive, analyze, categorize, reason, and decide. If provided with enough information, we can solve almost any problem. But our minds do not have the necessary information to answer such questions as:
- "Where do I come from?"
- "Who am I?"
- "Where do I go when I die?"
- "Is there a purpose to life?"
- "Why is the human condition filled with suffering, sickness, and unhappiness?"

Our inability to answer these questions creates anxiety in us. In an attempt to alleviate our anxiety, many of us look to religion. Religion allows us to express our spirituality, and look beyond restraints of logic and reason for answers to our questions.

Many people believe in their experiences of intuition and precognition. Some people also claim to obtain revelations from God. These communications from God to the human mind usually occur during meditation or prayer. For people who experience revelations, it is evident that there is a greater energy beyond what we perceive in the physical world. If the mind can connect to this energy and transcend the body, then it is possible that something of the mind is able to survive in some form after the death of the body.

> *Establishing spiritual harmony gives us the ability to live a happier and more productive life.*

In today's fast-paced technological society, we often feel alienated from the world around us, from nature, other people, and our own spirituality. Modern-day life and stresses dull our sensitivity and distract us with more pressing practical concerns. Yet as our feelings of alienation grows, we become more and more ill at ease with a mechanical, monotonous, and superficial culture. Increasing anxiety can deteriorate the image we have of ourselves; in other words, it can damage our identity.

A spiritual quest is necessary to answer our questions of identity and purpose. We must strive to discover our true selves, and celebrate our connection with humanity and the Divine.

The Proofs of God

Many philosophers and theologians throughout the ages have tried to demonstrate or refute the existence of God. St. Thomas Aquinas, in the thirteenth century, proposed the following arguments as the ways through which the mind can unequivocally reason the existence of God:

1 Argument for the "unmoved mover": The world is made of motion. Everything we know is moved by the action of something else. This something else must therefore have been put into motion itself at some previous time. If we continue to trace back to the first mover, we see that the first mover must be something which was capable of putting itself into motion. This could only be God.
2 Argument for the "first cause": Everything we know is caused or brought into being by another: the pot is

fashioned by a potter, who came to be from the union of his parents, who were the product of their parents and so forth. Everything can be traced back through a chain of causes to the first cause: God.
3 Argument for time and eternity: Everything on earth (even mountains and rivers) eventually disappears. Even stars are born and collapse. We can reason that our own planet will one day cease to exist. If all things are caused by another, there must be at least one eternal cause which is independent of time, birth or death: God.
4 Argument for a goal: Everything we know of in the world is in motion towards a goal. In the same way that a man directs an arrow toward a target, there must be a divine intelligence to direct all things towards their goals: God.

Why a Religion?

Looking back upon the great living religions – those which were founded hundreds, even thousands of years ago, and still have millions of followers – we see the many ways in which they are beneficial to society:

- Gods, spirits and religious myths have been the source of many artistic masterpieces, such as the cave paintings of Lascaux in France, Michaelangelo's frescoes, Mozart's Requiem and the Reclining Buddha of Sri Lanka.
- A code of behavior based on the will of God provides structure and direction in life. All known religions have rules of morality to guide our relationships with others in society.
- Religion brings people together and creates a form of social commitment between them, even as each pursues his or her individual religious path.
- The rituals of religion mark the passage of time and validate the changes and events in life. The sharing of joy and sorrow gives people a sense of self-worth, and increases community cohesiveness and pride.
- Rituals and prayer give believers a sense of control over their environment. Today, as was true in primitive societies, one can beseech God for assistance. If God does not respond (by not sending rain, healing the sick, providing solutions to financial difficulties etc.), it is

thought to be due to one's own lack of faith or incompetence in performing a ritual. Our feeling of control, however unwarranted, does reduce anxiety.

Religion binds people to God by celebrating the Spirit in each person, and its connection to the greater Spirit, of which we all are part. Recognizing our connection to God gives us a sense of belonging, purpose, and common destiny.

Common Elements of Religions

Religions are like different rays of the same light, separated as the light travels through a prism, each appears a different color and quality.

The religions of the world, from the prehistoric past to the present, are structurally similar in many ways. Their practices require prayer, worship, and other rituals.

Rituals

Religious rituals are used to communicate with God in worship or supplication, or to acknowledge events which are part of the divine plan.

- A ritual common to all known religions is sacrifice or offerings. Worshipers endure some hardship or give something they value to pay homage to their God. The Aztecs sacrificed prisoners of war, believing that the Gods needed blood to maintain their strength. Catholics abstain from eating meat at certain times of year. Many cultures give offerings of food and other necessities to their priests, who accept the offerings on behalf of God.
- Most religions hold regular public services, in which rituals are performed for the purpose of worship. Attendance is often required by religious law or tradition.

- Many religious rituals celebrate the change of seasons and other natural occurrences. In primitive agricultural societies, rituals were performed to bring rain and to ensure a bountiful harvest. Hunters ritually entreated the gods for plentiful game.
- Other rituals celebrate the important events of human life, and serve as *rites of passage*. They help to diminish one's anxiety as he or she prepares to take up a new role in life, and officially announce the new role to the community. Most religions ritually commemorate the birth and naming of children, puberty or some other passage into adulthood, marriage, and death. Many cultures have rituals of *ordination* for persons who assume a religious office or other important community role.
- Rituals also celebrate important dates in the history of the religion, such as the birth or death of its founder and other important persons; visions, miracles, and other profound events; and times of great suffering or triumph.

Ethical Training

Instruction in religious morality reduces the mind states of greed, anger, hate, lust etc. This allows greater concentration on higher level religious teachings.

Mind Training

Regaining control over the mind is essential to ascending to higher levels of religious awareness. The mind is the source of all pleasure and suffering. The mind can be controlled by various attention techniques such as meditations.

Parables

Religions rely on parables to explain their origins, beliefs and customs. Creation parables explain the origin of the world, its laws of operation, and the role of humans in it. Many rituals and customs are parables or symbolic reenactments of events. The custom of placing the star on the top of the Christmas tree, for example, signifies a star which was said to appear on the night of the birth of Jesus Christ.

Mysticism

An element of mysticism is common to all religions. All known religions have procedures for obtaining control over events or manipulating natural and supernatural forces.
- Ritual imitation of mythical figures can fill a person with their powers.
- Objects that belonged to, or were closely associated with a sacred spot or person can still hold power.
- Certain objects, often called *fetishes*, are thought to hold powers because of their appearance or origin. Relics from saints and martyrs are among these. The Christian priest performs a ritual which imbues the communion wafer with the sacred powers of Christ's body.

Prayer & Worship

Some form of prayer is used in all religions to address sacred spirits or gods. Prayers can contain some or all of the following elements: adoration, confession, promises, thanksgiving, and supplication. They can follow a ritual formula or be like an informal conversation with God, can be spoken or sung aloud (in groups or alone) or recited only in one's mind.

All religions entail worship. While some religions worship objects as sacred in themselves, others worship the Spirit or sacred energy inherent in an object. Still other religions worship a more abstract sacred force, of which certain objects are only symbols or tools to focus the mind. The God or sacred energy of these religions is more powerful and transcendent than the others.

Sacred Places

Sacred places are believed to help us concentrate on our spiritual endeavors. Some special event may have happened there, or a sacred object may be kept there. (These include the grotto of Lourdes, the Bo tree of the Buddha, birthplaces of saints and prophets, relics of saints).

Places of Worship

Places of worship (churches, temples and mosques) are chosen or built in order to establish a sacred place, conducive to meditation, prayer, or illumination.

Sacred Texts and Scriptures

These are considered to be divinely inspired. They may have been orally transmitted for thousands of years before being written down, and therefore remain anonymous. The Vedas and the Old Testament are examples. Or they may have been told to a prophet through revelation, or be a compilation of discourses, prayers, hymns, and myths. The Koran and the Guru Grant Sahib of the Sikhs are examples. These texts often explain the relationship of the creator and its creation, as well as the rules of spiritual and social behavior.

Clerics and Holy People

These individuals devote their lives to their religion. They can be ministers, spiritual leaders, readers and interpreters of sacred texts, counselors, or intermediaries between lay-persons and God. They may also live as hermits and devote themselves entirely to prayer.

The Great Living Religions

Learning about spiritual beliefs and practices other than our own teaches us respect, compassion, and love for humanity.

Today there are hundreds of religions in practice throughout the world. Of the major religions, four were founded in India: Hinduism, Buddhism, Jainism and Sikhism. Taoism and Confucianism originated in China. Shinto was the religion of Japan. Iran gave birth to Zoroastrianism. The Near and Middle East saw the founding of Judaism, Christianity and Islam.

Of all these religions, Hinduism, Shinto and Judaism have existed for so long that we have no historical documentation of their origins, although Abraham is believed to be the founder of Judaism, and the sages of India (known as *Rishis*, are said to have created Hinduism from the direct inspiration of God. Even less is known about the origins of Shinto.

Confucianism and Zoroastrianism take their names directly from their founders: Confucius, the sixth century BC philosopher who preached ethical conduct and devotion to family and society; and Zoroaster, a Persian religious teacher from the sixth or seventh century, BC. Jainism, Buddhism, and Christianity refer to the titles given to their founders: a Jain is a conqueror who overcomes in a spiritual way, as did its founder, Vardhamana. Buddha, the Enlightened One, was born Siddartha Gautama, and Jesus became known as Christ, the Anointed One.

Taoism, Sikhism, and Islam refer to a certain path prescribed by the religion itself. Tao is Chinese for "the Way," implying the harmonious way the universe exists, and the way humans should live, in harmony with all things. A Sikh is, literally, a disciple; one who follows the religious path of Sikhism. Islam is an Arabic word which means "submission." In terms of the religion, it means "Submission to the Will of Allah."

Religious Affiliations of the People of the World
33%	Christians	
	Catholic	19%
	Orthodox	3%
	Protestant	11%
17%	Moslems	
13%	Hindus	
6.5%	Buddhists	
1%	Taoists	
0.5%	Jews	
9%	other religions	
20%	non-religious	

Hinduism

Hinduism is always changing and adapting to its cultural environment. It is not so much one religion, as a whole family of faiths shared by the many people of India.
- Hindus can choose from many systems and practices. They can select to belong to a temple and become members of a congregation, or to establish a direct mystical connection with the Brahma, the name of God.
- A Hindu can choose a quiet lifestyle of asceticism and contemplation, or a more active life as a householder and member of society.
- Because Hinduism is extremely complicated, a personal *Guru*, or spiritual master, is of great importance in practicing the proper devotions and following the path to God through this religious system.

The Sacred Hindu Texts

The oldest Hindu sacred writings are the *Vedas* or "Sacred Knowledge."
- The Vedas are made up of four parts, which together form the *Samhita*, and are believed to have been written between 3100 BC and 2000 BC.
- These texts are the oldest religious scriptures known today.
- Three of the Vedas are books of hymns, and the fourth book contains magic spells.
- The Vedas were later supplemented by the *Brahmas*, which explained the proper uses of the hymns and prayers.
- The Forest Books, *Aramyakas*, were created for those who chose to live in isolated areas for the purpose of devotion to meditation and prayer.
- Philosophical treatises known as the *Upanishads* are the most recent addition to the Vedas. They elaborate on the use of hymns, and explain the relationship between Brahma and the individual soul or *atman*. The Upanishads date from around 900 AD.

- The Vedas and the commentaries are considered to be the original, divinely inspired texts of Hinduism. The Vedas describe the belief in Brahma, the absolute God, who can be reached through the invocation of his manifestations as the numerous Hindu Gods, and by the use of special ceremonies, prayers, and sounds. (See *Mantras*.)
- In the *Bhagavad-Gita*, (a poem that is part of a longer epic) the method for achieving oneness with God is revealed in a dialogue between Lord Krishna and Prince Arjuna. It entails proper knowledge (Jnana), pure devotion (Bhakti) breath control (Prana Yana), and right action (Karma).
- The Upanishads, which take the form of a dialogue, were probably written at least in part by members of the military caste, *Kshatriyas*, who were second only to the Brahmans. The Upanishads portrayed women as equal to men in their ability to succeed in spiritual endeavors. They also advocated asceticism, at a time when many Brahmans retreated into the forests.

Asceticism and Moksha

Asceticism is greatly valued in Hinduism, where self-inflicted deprivation and renunciation is considered equal to the sacrifices made at the altar. It is up to the individual to choose modes of renunciation that are compatible with his or her situation in life; however, certain renunciations are commonly expected:
- Intoxicants, illicit sex, and all types of violence are abhorred.
- Vegetarianism is strongly encouraged, both as an austerity and to avoid harm to animals.

Asceticism and meditation together can free one to move from the material body into the realm of the spirit. There one can join with Brahma, the all-inclusive and eternal being, with whom humans long for reunification.
- Union with God provides deliverance from life and its pain.

- All manifested things are not completely real; they constitute *maya*, (illusion) as opposed to Brahma, the only real, undeniable, and eternal being.
- The human soul is part of the eternal soul of Brahma: it is *Sat-Cit-Ananda*, Being, Consciousness and Bliss, and as such it longs for mystical union with God.
- Material things are of only passing value: they cannot be shared without decreasing; they cannot be kept after death; even during one's lifetime, riches, health or happiness are easily lost. Material wants are never satisfied: the more one acquires, the more one desires.
- Spiritual attainments, however, are of eternal value. Once acquired, they remain with one and assure a better situation in the next life, as explained in the Law of Karma. If one shares spiritual values, he or she gains in generosity, compassion, and mercy.
- Only total absorption in spiritual practice can guarantee *Moksha*, liberation from the material plane. Such liberation will automatically bring consciousness of one's real being, and consequently, Bliss (Ananda).
- Moksha is the highest and most sought-after goal of any Hindu. By attaining Moksha, one experiences Nirvana, the sweetness of which cannot be described by words. The cycle of rebirth ends, and one escapes the Law of Karma.

The Law of Karma

The universe goes through cycles of creation, followed by total destruction, when the souls of all beings leave their bodies and remain suspended until a new cycle begins.
- During any cycle, the soul migrates from body to body after each death.
- One can be reborn in any other body – vegetable, animal or human – and into any caste.
- According to the Law of Karma, all of a being's thoughts, words and actions in one life have direct and absolute influence upon its future incarnations.

The Caste System

The four original castes of Indian society gradually separated into hundreds of sub-castes. The lowest group of people was pushed out of the castes altogether: they became known as *untouchables*. The Law of Karma gave a sort of moral justification to the caste system: No one should feel pity for people of the lower castes or the untouchables, because their situations were the direct result of their thoughts and actions in past lives. They were only getting what they deserved.

The Hindu God

Brahma is the eternal, undefinable supreme God, who also manifests himself as Vishnu, Krishna, Shiva, and a number of other Gods and Goddesses. The Hindus believe in only one God, yet they worship the many manifestations of God. This is similar to the Christian doctrine of the Holy Trinity, in which the Father, Son, and Holy Spirit are different and simultaneous manifestations of the one God.

Quotes on Bhakti and the Availability of God, from the *Bhagavad–Gita*

The Blessed Lord said:

Attach your mind to Me; put your trust in Me; listen how you may come to know Me in my entirety with all doubt dispelled.

These sacred writings are derived from the wisdom of experiences I shall proclaim to you, leaving nothing unsaid.

Knowing these things, never again will any other thing remain that needs to be known.

Only one in a thousand will strive for self-perfection; and even among those few who strive, but one, maybe, will come to know Me as I really am.

Eight fold divided is my Nature – thus: Earth, water, fire, air, space, mind, soul and the ego.

This is the lower, but I also have a higher Nature. You must know this also.

And this Nature is seen as the life by which this universe is kept in being.

From these two Natures all beings take their origin. Be very sure of this.
In the whole universe the origin of the dissolution too am I.
Higher than Me there's nothing whatsoever.
On me the universe is strung like clustered pearls upon a thread.
In water I am the flavor, in sun and moon the light, in all the sacred words I'm the sound. In man I am.
Pure fragrance in the earth I am. A flame's beginning in the fire. In life I am in all contingent beings, in ascetics their fierce austerity.
Know that I am the eternal seed of all contingent beings: reason in the rational, glory in the glorious I am...

Quotes from the Katha Upanisad

God made sense so that it looks outward. Man therefore looks outward and not into himself. On occasion an adventurous man, seeking immortality, looks inward and finds himself.

The foolish man chases pleasure and sinks into the entanglements of death. But the wise man, seeking the truth, does not chase after things that die.

God through whom we see, taste, smell hear and feel knows everything. Our Greater Self within is with God.

The wise man meditates on the all knowing Greater Self within and comes to understand waking and sleeping and he goes beyond sorrow. He knows that the individual self in the Greater Self and he knows that there in nothing to fear.

The wise man knows that He himself was born in the beginning out of meditation, before water was created, and enters every heart and lives in all the elements. The infinite Power, the source of all power, manifests itself as life. It enters every heart, living there among the elements, that is Self.

The Fire hidden in the fire-stick like a baby in the womb, worshipped with offerings, that Fire is Self.

He who causes the sun to rise and set and to whom all powers give homage, He that has no master, this is Self.

That which is here is forever. He who thinks different wanders from death to death.

Tell your mind that there is but One; he who divides the One, wanders from death to death.

When that Person in the heart, no bigger than a dot is known as maker of past and future, what more is there to fear? That is Self.

That Person, no bigger than a dot, burning like a flame without smoke, maker of past and future, the same yesterday, today and tomorrow, that is Self.

Just as rain upon a mountain top runs down the slope, the man that has not seen the truth of Self runs after them everywhere.

The Self of the wise man remains pure; pure water poured into pure water.

Quotes from the Mandukya Upanisad

Om! – this syllable is this whole world.

The past, the present, the future – everything is just the word Om. And whatever transcends past, present, and future – that, too, is just the word Om.

For truly, everything here is Brahman (God) and self is also Brahman. Self can be divided into four parts.

The first is the waking state, and it is the most common. It is outwardly cognitive, seeming to have seven limbs and nineteen mouths, and enjoying the gross parts of life.

The second is the dreaming state, inwardly cognitive and inwardly seeming to have seven limbs and nineteen mouths, and enjoying the exquisite dreams.

The third is the deep sleep state where man feels no desire and creates no dream, just a unified awareness consisting of bliss whose mouth is a cognitive mass.

The fourth is the Lord of all. This is the all-knowing. This is the inner controller. This is the source of all, for this is the origin and the end of beings.

Not inwardly cognitive, not outwardly cognitive, not both cognitive, not a cognitive mass, unseen and which there can be no dealing, ungraspable with no distinctive mark, not-thinkable with no designation, the essence of the assurance of which is the state of being with the Self, the cessation of development, tranquil, benign, One without a second.

This is the Self with regard to the word Om, with regard to its four elements.

Buddhism

Buddhism came about as an effort to understand the nature of life and the suffering of the human existence. Westerners often believe that Buddhists do not believe in God, but this is not true. Buddhism does not have a set concept of God because it holds that one particular concept would be too limiting. Buddhists believe that such a limited view could not do justice to the absolute God. This absolute God is beyond the concepts of our human mind. They believe that a limited concept of God can only show relative truths, and not the real truth of God that is absolute and beyond logic.

The Buddha's Life

Buddhism was founded by Siddartha Gautama, who became known as the Buddha, the Enlightened One. Siddartha was born in 563 BC in the city of Kapilavastu, Northern India. He was the son of a king. His father was told by a diviner that the young Siddartha would either become the greatest king of all India, or he would give up the worldly life altogether. His father took great pains to ensure that his young son would not encounter any distressing sight that could lead him to renounce his great and glorious destiny.

Yet on an outing to the nearby village, young Siddartha saw a very old and frail man. Another time he saw a sick and infirm man. On a third outing he saw a corpse, and so the young prince came to know of the universal human fate of old age, disease, and death. On a fourth outing however, Siddartha encountered a holy man, devoid of all luxury or even comfort, who seemed, none the less, totally content.

Siddartha continued to live a princely life, and was married at the age of sixteen to a distant cousin. Yet he was more and more attracted to the thought of leaving his household to pursue a spiritual quest. In his late twenties, Siddartha left home to begin a life of intense renunciation, which he would follow for six years.

Siddartha studied with various spiritual teachers and began a period of asceticism so severe that he became very emaciated and nearly died. Yet he did not feel any closer to enlightenment. Finally realizing that the path of starvation and denial would bring death sooner that enlightenment, he gave up his asceticism. This caused his companions to abandon and denounce him.

Left alone, Siddartha started a quiet meditation at a place now called *Bodhi-Gaya*, under a fig tree which became known as the *Bodhi tree*, or tree of knowledge. Through his meditation, Gautama suddenly received the revelation that became the Buddhist doctrine.

> *The essence of the Buddhist doctrine is that all suffering in life is due to the never-ending desires which cannot be fulfilled.*

After his enlightenment, the Buddha faced a crucial decision: to enter Nirvana, or to remain on earth and help others to attain enlightenment. He chose to remain. The Buddha went to Benares, where he found his companions again. He won them over and they became his first disciples.

The order of monks grew rapidly, and was governed by definite rules:
- The initiates pledged to take refuge in the Buddha, the *Dharma* (Truth), and the *Sangha* (Order).
- The monks wore yellow robes and shaved their heads.
- They carried begging bowls, with which to beg for their food, and spent most of the day in meditation.

The Buddha continued to preach to a growing number of disciples, monks and nuns, including his son and many of his relatives. At the age of eighty, he died in the town of Kusinara. Buddha left his doctrine to those who came after him, and enjoined them to work out their own salvation.

The Buddhist Doctrine

Release from the pain of life, with its unending and unfulfilled desires, requires that one break the bonds of wrong attitudes and beliefs. One must then accept the *Four Noble Truths*, and live by the tenets of the *Eight-fold Path*. According to the Buddha, this would assure enlightenment.

Bonds that Need to be Broken to Ensure Salvation
- The three intoxications: greed, hatred, and ignorance.
- The five hindrances: desire for sense-pleasing, ill will, sloth, restlessness, and doubt.
- The ten fetters: belief in the existence of the self, doubt, trust in ceremonies and rituals, lust, anger and ill will, desire for rebirth in another form, desire for rebirth without form, pride, self-righteousness, and ignorance.

The Four Noble Truths
1 Life is filled with suffering from birth to death.
2 This suffering is caused by a ignorance of the nature of reality and attachment and craving for worldly things.
3 Suffering will stop when one learns to overcoming ignorance and attachment.
4 The way to end suffering is by following the Eight–fold Path.

The Eight–fold Path
We can learn end suffering by following the Eight–fold Path:
1 Right belief (in the Four Noble Truths).
2 Right aspiration (purpose; overcoming sensuality and desires, and the belief in the sanctity of all life).
3 Right speech (speaking kindly and truthfully to all).
4 Right conduct (acting skillfully and righteously).
5 Right means of livelihood (earning one's living without harm to others).
6 Right effort (remaining alert and being discriminating).
7 Right mindfulness (controlling one's thoughts and emotions).

8 Right meditation (daily meditation that will lead to enlightenment).

Nirvana
Nirvana is the final goal of the Buddhist path. It is release from all illusion with its inherent suffering. Nirvana is an enlightened state in which greed, hatred, and ignorance are no longer in control.

Divisions of Buddhism
As Buddhism spread through India, it divided into two distinct traditions: *Mahayana* Buddhism, the greater raft, and *Theravada* Buddhism, the lesser raft, which follows the teachings of the elders. These divisions were based on the way in which one was believed to reach Nirvana: alone, on a raft only big enough for one; or on the greater raft, with many other people.

Buddhism was also influenced by the countries to which it spread. It branched into *Zen* Buddhism in Japan, and into *Lamaism* in Tibet.

The Lesser Raft
In traditional or Theravada Buddhism, the all-important monk preaches self-reliance in the path towards enlightenment. It is believed that the Buddha has entered into Nirvana, and can no longer help anyone.
- Meditations on love, pity, joy, impurity, and serenity are practiced daily.
- Buddha images are part of the Theravada tradition.
- Buddha is revered as a divine, perfect, and all-knowing being who came to Earth to preach the way. He has appeared on Earth many times before, and will return in the future.
- Sanctuaries exist for the purpose of pilgrimages, and special holidays are celebrated, principally on the Buddha's birthday, the day of his enlightenment, and the day of his death.
- In countries where Hinayana Buddhism predominates, most men are expected to spend three months of each year in monastic life.

- Yet for all the prayer, devotion, meditation and celebration, Theravadan Buddhists do not expect divine intervention. The name Hinayana itself, the lesser raft, represents the individual crossing the river to enlightenment alone, guided by no one, and guiding no one else.

The Greater Raft

Mahayana Buddhism believes that the greater raft, piloted by the Buddha, transports large numbers of devotees simultaneously. Mahayana Buddhism became popular in Northern India.
- In this tradition, Buddha is a divine being who has come to earth out of compassion for humans.
- Buddhas have come before, and those who will appear in the future are *Boddhisattvas*, (an individual who has attained perfect enlightenment.)
- Or enlightenment is the standard that Buddhist should strive for.

Mahayana followers profess that Buddha himself, in his private teachings, described three kinds of Buddhas who can help one attain salvation:
- The *Manushi* Buddhas appear on earth, like Gautama himself.
- The Boddhisattvas exist in great numbers, and answer the appeals of mortals, like angels of compassion.
- The *Dhyani* Buddhas reside in heaven to inspire contemplation and peace.

Mahayana Buddhism spread into China, where it assimilated parts of Taoism and Confucianism, the religious systems already there. Later the Buddhist ideals of humanitarianism spread to Korea and Japan. China and Japan host a great pantheon of Boddhisattvas, including Goddesses of Mercy who parallel the Virgin Mary of the Catholic church.

In Tibet, Buddhism took on a third form. Here it is called Lamaism, after its high priest, the *Dalai Lama* or *Mantrayana* Buddhism, due to the importance of the mantras in the devotional service.

In Tibet, the Buddha of Mercy has a consort: Tara. From this arose *Tantra Yana* or the Buddhism of Tantra:
- Tantra holds a quasi-magical character, with elements of secrecy and the vital role of the spiritual master or guru.
- Sacred rites involving the body and mind must be performed in order to reach illumination. Such rites can include chanting mantras, consuming certain foods and beverages, and even performing sex acts.
- The belief that all things are produced by the union of male and female forces leads to the use of sex as an affirmation of the Oneness. Similarly, each God has his consort, and it is in union with his consort that he achieves the utmost power.
- Tara is generally the symbol of compassion, purity and piety, qualities which the Buddhist woman is expected to exemplify. Yet she can also take on other aspects, such as the red Tara, who symbolizes wealth, or the yellow Tara, the embodiment of anger.

Zen Buddhism

Another form of Buddhism prevalent in Japan is Zen Buddhism, which uses meditation to attain sudden insight into the nature of the self.
- As in Hinayana Buddhism, salvation is an individual and solitary endeavor.
- Zen emphasizes practice and personal enlightenment rather than scripture study.
- Zen teachings are passed orally from Master to students.
- To achieve sudden awakening, one must get away from thinking in terms of duality, and go beyond the intellect and its questions.
- Sometimes a *koan*, or seemingly illogical problem, is given to students to encourage the necessary and sudden shift in thinking.
- Contemplation of nature and humanity is paramount to the practice of Zen; this has given rise to the celebrated Japanese art forms of poetry, flower arranging, decorative arts and the tea ceremony.

The Great Way
by Sengstan, Third Zen Buddhist Patriarch

*The Great Way is not difficult
for those who have no preferences.
When love and hate are both absent
everything becomes clear and undisguised.
Make the smallest distinction, however,
and heaven and earth are set infinitely apart.
If you wish to see the truth
then hold no opinions for or against anything.
To set up what you like against what you dislike
is the disease of the mind.
When the deep meaning of things is not understood
the mind's essential peace is disturbed to no avail.*

*The Way is perfect like vast space
where nothing is lacking and nothing is in excess.
Indeed, it is due to our choosing to accept or reject
that we do not see the true nature of things.
Live neither in the entanglements of outer things,
nor in inner feelings of emptiness.
Be serene in the oneness of things
and such erroneous views will disappear by themselves.
When you try to stop activity to achieve passivity
your very effort fills you with activity.
As long as you remain in one extreme or the other
you will never know Oneness.*

*Those who do not live in the single Way
fail in both activity and passivity,
assertion and denial.
To deny the reality of things
is to miss their reality.
To assert the emptiness of things
is to miss their reality.
The more you talk and think about it,
the further astray you wander from the truth.
Stop talking and thinking,
and there is nothing you will not be able to know.
To return to the root is to find the meaning,
but to pursue appearances is to miss the source.*

*At the moment of inner enlightenment
there is a going beyond appearance and emptiness.*

*The changes that appear to occur in the empty world
we call real only because of our ignorance.
Do not search for the truth;
only cease to cherish opinions.*

*Do not remain in the dualistic state;
avoid such pursuits carefully.
If there is even a trace
of this and that, of right and wrong,
the Mind essence will be lost in confusion.
Although all duality come from the One,
do not be attached even to this One.
When the mind exists undisturbed in the Way,
nothing in the world can offend,
and when a thing can no longer offend,
it ceases to exist in the old way...*

*With a single stroke we are freed from bondage;
nothing clings to us and we hold to nothing.
All is empty, clear, self-illuminating,
with no exertion of the mind's power.
Here thought, feeling, knowledge, and imagination
are of no value.
In this world of Suchness
there is neither self nor other-than-self.*

*To come directly into harmony with this reality
just simply say when doubts arise, "Not two."
In this "not two" nothing is separate,
nothing is excluded.
No matter when or where,
enlightenment means entering this truth.
And this truth is beyond extension or
diminution in time or space;
in it a single thought is ten thousand years.
Emptiness here, Emptiness there,
but the infinite universe stands
always before your eyes.
Infinitely large and infinitely small;*

*no difference, for definitions have vanished
and no boundaries are seen.
So too with Being and non-Being.
Don't waste time in doubts and arguments
that have nothing to do with this.*

*One thing, all things:
move among and intermingle,
without distinction.
To live in this realization
is to be without anxiety about non-perfection.
To live in this faith is the road to non-duality
Because the non-dual is one with the trusting mind.*

*Words! The Way is beyond language,
for in it there is
    no yesterday
    no tomorrow
    no today.*

Taoism

    Taoism began in China around 500 BC. It has since influenced every aspect of Chinese culture.
    The object of Taoism is to move closer to the divine way of life. The Taoist often avoids the worldly pursuits of money and power and devotes himself or herself to more fully understanding the Tao.
    Taoism teaches that everything is basically one, despite the appearance of differences. It also states that problems arise only when people lose sight of this oneness. This concept is shown in the principle of yin/yang.
    Yin forces are described as yielding, moving inward, darkly colored and concentrating. They are symbolized as feminine forces. Yang forces are described as confrontive, moving outward, expansive, lightly colored and are considered masculine. And the Universe is recognized as being formed of yin and yang forces in balance. This is represented by a circle divided into two half by an S-shaped

line. One half of the circle is black and the other half is white. The white and black dots represent that yin contains an element of yang, and yang contains an element of yin.

Yin–Yang Symbol

Tao Te Ching

The Tao Te Ching was said to be written about 2500 years ago in China by a man named Lao Tzu. *Tao* means path, way or truth. *Te* is power, and *Ching* means book. Tao Te Ching thus is translated *The Book on the Way and the Power*. The Tao Te Ching is short, (only 5280 Chinese characters) yet it is one of the greatest and most influential books ever written.

From chapter 1
The Tao that can be told of is not the Absolute Tao.
The names that can be given are not Absolute Names.
Naming anything relegates it to being a material thing
And not the creation of the Mother of all Things.
Therefore:
Reduce needs in order to see the Secret of Life.
Yet also live with passion in order to see its manifest forms.
Both actions are the same
but they are given different names.

They may both be called the Cosmic Mystery.

From chapter 2
When people know beauty as beauty then there also arises ugliness.
When people know good as good then there also arises evil.
So:
Being and non-being inter depend in growth
Difficult and easy inter depend in completion
Long and short inter depend in contrast
High and low inter depend in position
Tones and voice inter depend in harmony
Front and behind inter depend in company.
Therefore the man of wisdom:
Manages affairs with non interference
Preaches the doctrine without words.
All things flourish without interruption
He gives them life, but does not take possession of them.
He accomplishes but claims no credit.
Because he claims no credit
then credit cannot be taken away.

From chapter 4
Tao is called the Great Power, empty yet inexhaustible!
Fathomless it gives birth to infinite worlds.
It is always present within you.
You can use it any way you want.

From chapter 9
Stretch a bow to the very full and you will wish you had stopped in time.
Temper a sword-edge to its very sharpest, and the edge will not last long.
When gold and jade fill your hall, you will not be able to keep them safe.
To be proud with honor is to sow the seeds of one's downfall.
Retire when your work is done.
Such is the way of the Tao.

From chapter 11
Thirty spokes unite at the hub.
From their loss of individuality
arises the utility of the wheel.
Mold clay into a jar,
and from its not-being (hollowness)
arises the utility of the jar.
Cut out doors and windows in a house,
from their emptiness arises the utility of the house.
Therefore by the existence of things we profit,
and from the non-existence of things we are served.

From chapter 16
Empty your mind of all thinking.
Contemplate peace in your being.
Watch the turmoil and activity of all things;
Observe the endless cycle as they eventually return to
their original state of repose.
Like vegetation that luxuriantly grows;
But returns to the roots and soil from which it sprang.

If you don't understand this reality
you fall into confusion and suffering.
However, when you are in accord with the source
you become impartial, tolerant and enlightened.
Being one with the wonder of Tao
life no longer seems to be a problem.
You can transcend all that life brings to you;
And your whole life is preserved from harm.

From chapter 25
Before the universe was born
there was something formless and perfect.
It is silent and empty, solitary and unchanging.
It is infinite and the Mother of all things.
For lack of a better name, it is called Tao.
It is everywhere, flowing through all things,
and always connects to the source.
Tao is great.
The Heaven is great.
Earth is great.

Man is great.
Man comes from Earth.
Earth comes from Heaven.
Heaven comes from Tao.
Tao is that which is.

From chapter 67
All the world says that teaching the Tao is folly.
Because it is great it resembles folly.
If it did not resemble folly
it would long ago have become petty.
I have three treasures, guard them and keep them safe.
The first is love.
The second is moderation.
The third is humility.
Through love one drops fear.
Through moderation one is ample.
Through not presuming to be first in the world,
one develops full growth.

From chapter 76
When man is born he is tender and weak,
At death he is hard and stiff.
When plants are alive, they are soft and flexible.
When they are dead they are brittle and dry.
Hardness and stiffness are the companions of death.
Softness and gentleness are the companions of life.
Therefore when an army is too stiff it will lose in Battle.
When a tree is hard, it will be cut down.
The big and strong position is low.
The gentle and weak position is high.

From chapter 78
There is nothing more yielding than water.
Yet the soft water overcomes the hardest rock.
Weakness overcomes strength,
and gentleness overcomes rigidity.

Judaism

Deuteronomy 6
Hear O Israel! The Lord our God, the Lord is One!
And you shall love the Lord your God with all your heart and with all your soul and with all your mind.
And set these words, which I command you today, upon your heart.
And teach them faithfully to your children and speak of them when you sit in your house and when you walk by the way and when you lie down and when you rise up.
Bind them as a sign upon your hand. Let them be a symbol before yore eyes. Inscribe them on the door-posts of your house and on your gates.

Jews base their monotheistic religion on the belief in an omnipotent and unknowable God named Yahweh. Yahweh created everything: space and time, light, humans and animals, the planets, the sun, and the stars. This is explained in *Genesis*, the first book of the Bible.

- Yahweh is a benevolent God, most often portrayed as a merciful and caring father figure. He is a God of love, which is directed towards his chosen people, the Jews.
- Because God cannot be seen, attained or directly experienced, the proof of his love for his people must be found in his gifts to them of the land of Israel, and his laws to guide their lives.
- No matter how bad one's situation or sorrow may be, faith in Yahweh is a source of hope: a meaning can be derived from any situation, and a solution can be found.
- In Judaism, the material world is not dismissed, but rather incorporated into the constant search for meaning. All aspects of the world are important, because even the body and nature are part of salvation, and can be inhabited by God.
- Because life is considered to be good, and human society worth participating in, Judaism gave rise to a positive attitude towards progress and the ability of humans to

change and improve their lives. Judaism has influenced both Christianity and Islam in this way.
- Humans are thought to be capable of self-direction; they have the ability to become almost Godlike, but they do not always have the strength or will to do so. They are created in the image of God, and can struggle to become sublime, yet they are frail and perishable, and easily led astray.
- Humans are seen as God's beloved children; God yearns for their love, and in turn they can be confident of always being accepted, loved and cared for by God.

Much of Western culture is influenced by Jewish thought.
- Our ideas about God and our moral values are shaped by Jewish ideology.
- Legal systems in the Western world are often based on Jewish philosophies.
- Both Islam and Christianity stem from Judaism.
- Our sciences, art, philosophy and other intellectual pursuits owe much to Jewish minds such as Albert Einstein and Sigmund Freud.

Abraham and the Origins of Judaism

Yahweh appeared to Abraham and made a special covenant with him. He made a promise of everlasting love and support for Abraham's people, and their descendants, as long as they continued to abide by His law.

Yahweh also promised Abraham a son. At the age of eighty-six, Abraham's son Ismael was born to his wife's slave girl, Hagar. When Abraham was one hundred, his son Isaac was born to his wife, Sarah, who was ninety years old at that time. Yahweh later demanded the life of Isaac as a sacrifice from Abraham as a test of faith. Because Abraham was willing to sacrifice even his son, Yahweh spared Isaac from death.

Chapter 3 The Great Religions

> *God demands the utmost obedience from his people, and their complete trust is ultimately rewarded.*

Abraham was the first Jew chosen by God. Since God's covenant with Abraham, the Jewish people believe that they are God's chosen people, and that they receive the eternal love of their God.

The Torah

The Torah contains all the religious writings of Judaism. Many of these writings were given to the Jewish people from God through revelations in words, and revelations in the history of the people themselves, through the acts of God. For example, God revealed to Abraham his covenant with the Jews. God led the Jews out of Egypt. He also revealed the *Ten Commandments* to Moses. The Torah contains all the following things, and much more.

- One part of the Torah is the *Talmud*. In the third century AD, the writings on Jewish civil and religious law were gathered to form the Talmud. It is composed of the *Mishnah*, which contains the laws themselves, and the *Gemara*, a collection of commentaries on the laws.
- These commentaries were written by different religious scholars, in Babylon and in Palestine.
- The Torah also contains the *Holy Scriptures*, known to Christians as the *Old Testament*..

The Ten Commandments

Over 600 commandments are found in the *Book of Leviticus* in the Bible. Of these, ten commandments are said to have been revealed to the prophet Moses by God himself. The Ten Commandments form the basis of the moral code of Judaism. They are listed as follows:

The Ten Commandments, from Exodus Chapter 20
Then God spoke saying all these words:

I am the Lord your God who brought you out of the land of Egypt, out of the house of bondage. You shall have no other gods before Me.

You shall not make yourself an idol or any likeness of anything that is in heaven above or on the earth beneath or in the water under the earth.

You shall not bow down or serve them; for I am a jealous God, visiting the iniquity of the fathers on the children, on the third and fourth generations of those who hate Me, but showing steadfast love and kindness to thousands, to those who love Me and keep My commandants.

You shall not take the name of the Lord your God in vain for the Lord will not leave him unpunished who takes His name in vain.

Remember the Sabbath day, to keep it holy. Six days you shall labor, and do all your work. But the seventh day is a Sabbath of the Lord your God. In it you will not do any work, you or your son or your daughter, your servant or your cattle or your sojourner who stays with you. In six days your Lord made heaven and earth, the sea, and all that is in them, and rested the seventh day. Therefore your Lord blessed the Sabbath day and made it holy.

Honor your father and your mother, that your days may be prolonged in the land which your Lord God gives you.

You shall not murder.

You shall not commit adultery.

You shall not steal.

You shall not bear false witness against your neighbor nor covet your neighbor's wife or his servant, or his ox or his donkey or anything that belongs to your neighbor.

The Hallowed Life

Psalm 23
The Lord is my shepherd; I shall not want.
He makes me lie down in green pastures,
He leads me beside still waters.
He restores my soul;
he guides me on paths of righteousness, for His name's sake.
Though I walk through the valley of the shadow of death,
I shall fear no evil, for You are with me.
Your rod and Your staff do comfort me.
You prepare a communion table before me in the presence of my enemies.
You anoint my head with oil, my cup overflows.
Surely goodness and mercy shall follow me all the days of my life;
And I will live in the house of the Lord forever.

Jewish teachings include many rules and rituals. These must be followed to ensure that one's daily life is sacred, or "true to the Torah." The practice of the rituals and observances has been tremendously relaxed in the Western world, but orthodox Jews still follow them in the strict, traditional manner.

- Prayers are said three times a day.
- A blessing must be said over every meal.
- All newborn males are circumcised, as a sign of God's covenant with the Jews.
- Marriage is sacred, because the union of man and woman brings forth children for the glory of God. Procreation in marriage is seen as the duty of all Jews.
- A good family life is believed to ensure happiness and longevity.
- Dietary laws are complex. For instance, one may eat cows but not camels, because cows are cloven-footed, whereas camels have a solid hoof. Aquatic animals can only be consumed if they have fins and scales. Scavengers such as bottom-feeding fish and shellfish are not permitted. Animal flesh and dairy products cannot be served

together, or from the same dishes. Animals must be killed quickly, followed by a ritual blood-letting.
- Food that is obtained or prepared according to Jewish dietary laws is said to be *kosher*.
- Being charitable and helpful to others is required of all Jews. Forgiving debts, tithing, giving alms, and so forth, are thought to be very pleasing to God.

The Proverbs Chapter 8 and 9
(The wisdom of Solomon the son of David.)
    Wisdom calls and understanding will come.

For wisdom is on the heights by the paths; beside the gates in front of town; at the entrance of the city wisdom calls aloud saying:

    To you O men I, wisdom, call so that simple people may understand prudence and that fools understand wisdom.

    Listen for I shall speak the truth and my words are righteous. There is nothing wicked or unright.

    My words are all plain to him who understands them and right to those who are willing to seek knowledge. Take my instruction instead of silver, and knowledge rather than gold. For wisdom is better than jewels, and all that you may desire cannot compared with it.

    I wisdom have created prudence, and I possess knowledge and reason.

    Reverence of God despises evil; pride, arrogance, evil ways, and perverse speech.

    I have counsel and sound wisdom; I have insight, I have strength.

    By me kings reign and rulers decree what is just. By me princes rule and nobles govern the earth.

    I love those who love me and those who seek me diligently will find me.

    Riches and honor are mine. My fruit is better than fine gold and my yield better than choice silver.

    I walk in the way of righteousness, in the midst of the paths of justice. That I may cause those that love me to have hope, and I will fill their treasuries.

    God created me as the first of his creations, before all of his works. I was established at the first before the beginning of the earth...

Chapter Nine

Wisdom has built its house and set up seven pillars.

Wisdom has slaughtered the beasts and mingled its wine, and prepared the table.

Wisdom has sent forth servants to call out upon the highest places and say, "Whosoever is simple, let him come to me."

He who lacks understanding, let him come and eat of my bread and drink of the wine I have mixes.

Leave simpleness and live and proceed in the way of insight and understanding.

He who corrects a bad man gets dishonor for himself, the wicked man is rebuked by his own blemish.

Criticize a bad man and he will hate you, but criticize a wise man and he will love you.

Give an opportunity to a wise man and he will be yet wiser; teach a righteous man and he will increase in wisdom.

Reverence of God is the beginning of wisdom; and knowledge of the righteous is understanding.

For by me your days will be multiplied and years of life will be added to you. If your are wise, you are wise for yourself and for your friends, but if you scoff you will bear it alone.

A foolish woman is boisterous. She knows no shame and sits at the door of her house calling those who pass by. She says, "He who is simple, let him come to me." And to those without understanding she says, "Stolen water is sweet, and bread eaten in secret is pleasant."

But he does not know that the mighty men perish with her and that her guests are in the depths of Sheol.

Awaken and do not abide in that place, and a multitude of years shall be added to your life.

Ecclesiastics Chapter 3

For everything there is a season and a time for every event under heaven:
A time to be born and a time to die;
A time to plant, and a time to harvest;
A time to kill, and a time to heal;
A time to tear down, and a time to build up;
A time to weep, and a time to laugh;

A time to mourn, and a time to dance;
A time to throw away stones, and a time to gather stones;
A time to embrace, and a time to shun embracing;
A time to seek, and a time to lose;
A time to keep, and a time to throw away;
A time to tear apart, and a time to sew together;
A time to be silent, and a time to speak;
A time to love, and a time to hate;
A time for war, and a time for peace.
What profit has the worker from his toils?

Islam

The word *Islam* means peace or surrender. To be Islamic is to be at peace with the will of Allah (God) or to surrender or submit to the will of Allah. The credo of Islam tells much about the religion: "*La ilaha illa Allah, Mohammedan rasul Allah,*" which means, "There is no God but God, Mohammed is His prophet."

Followers of Islam believe that there is no reality except God; and nothing but God exists. This belief dominates all aspects of life in Muslim countries, where laws and traditions are defined by the essential act of submission to Allah. Social interaction, family relationships, and private life are all subject to Muslim law.

The Life of Mohammed

Mohammed was born around the middle of the sixth century AD in Mecca, which is now the religious capital of Saudi Arabia. Mohammed grew up amidst political and spiritual chaos. There was little social cohesion, and no predominant legal system, moral code, or religion to regulate behavior.

Mohammed spent long hours in solitude, meditating and praying to Allah. He believed Allah was the only true God. Mohammed was concerned with the gross immorality of the teeming city, and hoped, through his prayers, to find a way to bring order to Mecca.

An angel appeared to Mohammed one night, and proclaimed to him that Allah was the only God. This night is known as the Night of Power, when peace fell over the entire earth.

Mohammed is said to be he last of a long line of Muslim prophets that include Moses and Jesus. Because he is the last, he is known as the Seal of the Prophets.

Mohammed received his first revelation when he was forty years old. The revelations continued over the next twenty-three years, sometimes through voices, sometimes as a single voice of the angel Gabriel. Often the revelations had a physical effect on Mohammed: he trembled, shook and cried out. These revelations were repeated by Mohammed and written down by his disciples on whatever was at hand. (There was no paper in Arabia at that time.)

Mohammed also told of having been flown to the highest realm of Heaven, where God himself entreated him to ask men to pray fifty times each day. Upon his descent, Mohammed met Moses, another prophet of Islam, who sadly acknowledged that the common man was incapable of such dedication to God. Mohammed was sent back several times to negotiate with God, until it was agreed that men would pray five times each day.

The Koran

The revelations of Mohammed were recorded by his disciples as verses. Verses were grouped into chapters or *surahs*, which together form the *Qu'ran* (or the *Koran*, as it is more commonly known), the holy book of Islam.

Because it came directly from God to Mohammed, and was transcribed immediately by the disciples of Mohammed, most Muslims believe in the absolute authenticity and infallibility of the Koran.
- The Koran is comprised of 114 surahs.
- It is meant to continue the teachings of the Old and New Testaments of the Bible.
- The Koran is best recited in its original Arabic, in which it has an especially rhythmic and poetic form.

- Unlike the Bible, historical events and heroes are usually only alluded to in the Koran, often out of context.
- In the Koran, God explains that he is forever forgiving, and always accessible: at any time a person can ask God for pardon, courage, and hope. There are no barriers between God and his people.
- God is absolute good, therefore his creation is also good. In this way, material possessions and wealth are considered to be good.
- Each Muslim has a unique path to follow, through which he can glorify God.
- Muslims believe that they are free; that their souls are free. Each individual is responsible for living right, or for going astray into forgetfulness and sin.
- No one can hide from God. On Judgment Day, everyone's actions will be recalled and examined, and people will be sent to Heaven (a cool place of waterfalls and fountains) or to Hell.
- The Koran speaks more about action than about ideas: its doctrine focuses upon the creation of the world by Allah, the freedom of the individual soul, the judgment to come, and most of all the omnipresent, omniscient, omnipotent nature of Allah.
- The Koran allows a man to have up to four wives, but today most unions in the Muslim world are monogamous.
- Women were enjoined to cover themselves and remain modest in appearance and behavior.

Islam does not preach pacifism. It advocates defending against "enemies." But it does not encourage conversion by force: only by right example and rational persuasion can non believers be brought to join the ranks of Islam.

Quotes from *The Koran*
Sura 9:1-10
By the white forenoon and the brooding night!
The Lord has neither forsaken you nor hates you and the last shall be better for you than the first.
The Lord will give to you and you will be satisfied.

Did He not find you an orphan and shelter you?
Did He not find you erring and guide you?
Did He not find you needy and suffice you?
As for the orphan, do not oppress him. And as for the beggar, scold him not. And as for your Lord's blessing, declare it.

Divisions in Islam

The most predominant groups are the *Shi'ites*, the *Sunnis*, and the *Sufis*. The Shi'ites are growing at a faster pace than other groups of Muslims, though Islam in general is growing rapidly. Today there are as many as 900 million Muslims.

Sunnis and Shi'ites

Sunnis, the traditionalists of Islam, comprise 85% of the Muslim population, while Shi'ites make up most of the remaining 15%. The Shi'ites differ with the Sunnis primarily on the basis of the order of succession of religious leadership. The Shi'ites believe that Mohammed's son-in-law, Ali, should have succeeded Mohammed directly, as the first supreme ruler of Islam. Instead, Ali's succession was delayed by three others. This is a division of historical character. The Shi'ites are much more fundamentalist in their beliefs, than are the Sunnis.

Sufis and Whirling Dervishes

The Sufis (from *suf* or wool, because they wear coarse woolen garments) arose in protest to the worldliness of later Islam. These mystics spend a great amount of time in the contemplation of Allah, hoping to know him during their lifetimes.
- The Sufis have developed their own rituals of worship involving music, dances, prayers and group repetition of the names of Allah. (Such repetitions are called *dhirk*, or remembrance.)
- Sufi poetry is known and admired throughout the world; it describes the longing for God.
- Through love and the opening of the heart to all creation, one encounters the Divine.

- Much symbolism is used to ascend towards God by degrees, until a complete extinction of the self is accomplished and separation from God disappears.
- Some Sufis claim direct knowledge of God, which goes against Muslim orthodoxy.
- Most Sufis receive their teaching from sheiks of a certain line of transmission of the tradition. The *whirling dervishes* of Kona in Turkey represent such a line.
- The dervishes use the practice of chanting and whirling as a religious act to grow towards God.

A Sufi Prayer
Towards the One
The perfection of love, harmony and beauty.
The only being.
United with all the illuminated souls,
who form the embodiment of the Master.
The Spirit of Guidance.

When you pray, enter the room as if for the last time.
When you love, give all that you are, saving none for yourself.

When you desire, desire me so completely that you are totally dependent that I come.
Every time you come to me, let part of you die in my heart.

Seek me, knowing there is no other way out.

Fall down and collapse in my presence so that I have no choice than to pick you up and carry you.

When you prepare to join me, say good-by to everything you know.
Every time you approach me be certain that you will never leave the same.

And when we have union, hope that no part of you survives to again separate, needing to pray, love, or desire again.

Have no thoughts, no trust, no vision of tomorrow, for it does not exist.

Spread yourself entirely before me, hiding nothing from my view.

Let your heart scream of peace, singing in the silence, until everything ends and I begin.

Christianity

The Old Testament prophecy of the appearance on Earth of the Messiah, who is the son of God, forms the basis of Christianity. Christians believe that it was fulfilled by the birth of Jesus of Nazareth two thousand years ago. Jesus, born in a stable in Nazareth, was called by his followers Christ, the Anointed One. At the time Jesus Christ was crucified, he had only a few hundred followers. Today there are about 1.6 billion Christians throughout the world.

The Life of Jesus

Around the age of thirty, Jesus started preaching. He also healed people with his touch, and raised the dead. Jesus was a Jew and, at first, his attraction was mostly to Jews by fulfilling what God had promised to Abraham, Isaac, and Jacob. A few years later, his teachings incurred the wrath of the Romans who had him executed as a criminal.

- Jesus taught that the day of judgment was approaching. He called for drastic changes in the way people lived so they might be judged worthy of going to Heaven.
- Through the use of parables, Jesus encouraged people to be compassionate and forgiving, and to care for the poor and sick. He believed that everyone was capable of choosing to live a peaceful and loving life.
- Jesus exemplified his teachings in his own life by loving and caring for everyone he met, refusing to use violence even to protect himself and by forgiving those who hurt him, even those who had him put to death.

- Jesus loved all people, regardless of class or condition.
- Christians believe that Jesus was resurrected after his death. Several days after his burial, his tomb was found empty. Some of his followers claim that he appeared before them in the flesh, with a solid body and apparent wounds from his crucifixion. Others said that he appeared to them as a spirit. After that he is believed to have ascended into heaven.
- While Islam and Judaism view Jesus as only one of God's chosen prophets, Christianity was founded on the belief that Jesus is actually the son of God, who came in fulfillment of the prophecies of the Old Testament.

The Gospels

The Bible is the sacred book of Christianity. It contains the *Old Testament*, written before Jesus, and the *New Testament*, which is based on the belief that Jesus was the prophesied Messiah and the son of God. The Old Testament is identical to the Scriptures of the Jewish Torah, and explains how God created the world.

The miracles and teachings of Jesus are known through the *Gospels*, which are said to be the accounts of four of his disciples: John, James, Mark, and Luke. The Gospels are a part of the New Testament, which also contains the *Acts of the Apostles*, the *Epistles*, and numerous writings and discourses added throughout the ages by philosophers and mystics, telling of their personal knowledge of God, or attempting to prove his existence.

Jesus' famous Sermon on the Mount (recounted in Matthew, Chapters 5 through 7) incorporates much of the essence of Christianity. (Another account of the Sermon on the Mount can be found in Luke, Chapters 11 and 12.)

The Sermon on the Mount

And when he saw the crowds he went up on a mound and sat down. His disciples assembled near him and he began to teach them saying,

Blessed are the humble for theirs is the kingdom of God.

Blessed are those who suffer for they will be comforted.

Blessed are the meek for they will inherit the earth.

Blessed are those who hunger and thirst for righteousness for they will be satisfied.

Blessed are the merciful for they will receive mercy.

Blessed are the pure in heart, for they will see God.

Blessed are the peacemakers, for they will be called the sons of God.

Blessed are those who have been persecuted for the sake of justice for the kingdom of God is theirs...

You have heard that it was said "An eye for an eye and a tooth for a tooth." But I say to you do not resist evil; but whoever strikes you on your right cheek, turn your other cheek to him also.

If anyone wants to sue you and take your shirt, let him have your coat also. Whoever compels you to carry a burden for a mile, go with him two.

Give to him who asks of you and do not deny he who wants to borrow from you.

You have heard that it was said "You shall love your neighbor and hate your enemy." But I say to you love your enemies and pray for those who persecute you so that you may be the son of your father in heaven; for it is He who causes the sun to rise on the evil and the good and sends rain to the righteous and the unrighteous.

For if you do good only to those who do good to you: Don't even tax collectors do the same?

And if you greet your brothers only what do you do more than others? Don't even the Gentiles do the same? Therefore be merciful, just as your Father is merciful.

Beware of doing your righteous acts in public to be noticed by others. When you give charity don't sound a trumpet as the hypocrites do in the churches and in the streets so that men will praise them.

But when you give charity do not let your left hand know what your right hand is doing. Keep your charity a secret; and your Father who sees in secret will compensate you.

And when you pray don't be like the hypocrites who love to stand and pray in the churches and street corners so that men will see them. But when you pray go into your inner room and shut the door and pray to your Father in secret and your Father will repay you.

And in your prayers don't use meaningless repetition as the non-believers do, for they suppose that they will be heard because of their many words. Don't be like them; for your Father knows what you need before you ask Him. But pray in this way:

> Our Father who art in heaven
> Hallowed be Thy name.
> Thy kingdom come
> Thy will be done,
> On earth as it is in heaven.
> Give us this day our daily bread
> And forgive our debts as we also have forgiven our debtors.
> And do not let us enter into temptation, but deliver us from evil. For Thine is the kingdom and the power and the glory forever. Amen.

If you forgive men their faults your Father in heaven will also forgive you. But if you do not forgive men, neither will your Father forgive your faults.

When you fast, do not look sad like a hypocrite; for they disfigure their faces, so that it may appear to men that they are fasting. Truly I say to you, that they have already received their reward. But as for you, when you fast wash your face and anoint your head, so that it may not appear to men that you are fasting, but to your Father who is in secret; and your Father who sees all will reward you.

Do not lay up treasures on earth, where moth and rust destroy and where thieves break in and steal. But lay up treasures in heaven where neither moth nor rust destroy, and where thieves do no break in or steal. For where your treasure is, there will your heart be also...

For this reason I say to you, do not be anxious for your life, for what you will eat, or what you will drink, or for what you will wear. Is life not more than food and the body more than clothing?

Look at the birds of the sky: They neither sow nor reap, they have no storeroom nor gather into barns and yet God feeds them. Are you not worth much more than they?

And which of you by being anxious can add a day to his life? And why do you worry about clothing? Consider the lilies of the field, how they grow: They neither toil nor *spin. Yet I say to you that even Solomon in all his glory did not clothe himself like one of these.*

Therefore if God so arrays the grass in the field, which is alive today and tomorrow is thrown into the furnace, won't he do much more for you, O men of little faith?

So don't be anxious about these things for your Father knows that you need all these things. But seek first the kingdom of God and all these things shall then be given to you. Do not be afraid for your Father has chosen to give you the kingdom. Therefore do not be worried about tomorrow; for tomorrow will care for itself.

Do not judge and you will not be judged. For in the same way that you judge people, you yourself will be judged.

And why do you look at the speck of sawdust in your brother's eye, but do not notice the log that is in your own eye? Or how can you say to your brother, "let me take the speck of sawdust out of your eye," and behold, the log is in your own eye? You hypocrite, first take the log out of your own eye, and then you will see clearly enough to take the speck out of your brother's eye.

Do not give what is holy to dogs, and do not throw your pearls before swine, lest they trample them under their feet, and turn and tear you to pieces.

Ask and you will receive; seek and you will find; knock and the door will be opened to you.

For everyone who ask receives, and he who seeks finds, and for he who knocks, the door will be opened. For what man is there among you, that when his son shall ask for a loaf would give him a stone? Or if he asked for a fish would give him a snake?

If you being man know how to give good gifts to your children, how much more does your Father in heaven give what is good to those who ask.

Therefore always treat others as you would have them treat you. This is the essence of the Law of the prophets.

Enter in through the narrow door, for wide is the door and broad is the road which leads to destruction, and many are those who travel on it. Narrow is the door, and difficult is the road which leads to life, and few are those who found it.

Be careful of false prophets who come to you in lamb's clothing, but within they are ravening wolves. You will know them by their fruits. Do they gather grapes from thorns or figs from thistles? So every good tree bears good fruit; but a bad tree bears bad fruit. A good tree cannot bear bad fruit; neither can a bad tree bear good fruit. Every tree which does not bear good fruit will be cut down and cast into the fire. Thus by their fruit you will know them.

It is not everyone who merely says to me, My Lord, my Lord, who will enter into the kingdom of heaven, but he enters who does the will of our Father in heaven. A great many will say to me in that day, My Lord, my Lord, did we not prophesy in your name and in your name cast out devils and in your name do many wonders? Then I will declare to them, I have never known you; keep away from me, you that work iniquity.

Therefore whoever hears these words of mine, and does them, he is like a wise man who built his house upon a rock. And the rain fell and the rivers overflowed and the winds blew, but the house did not fall because its foundations were laid upon a rock. And whoever hears these words and does them not, is like a foolish man who built his house upon sand. And the rain fell and the rivers overflowed and the winds blew and the house fell, and it was a great fall.

The Christian Church

After Jesus' death, his followers continued to spread his teachings as he himself had done. This formed the basis of the Christian Church, with a mission of converting all people to Christianity. It was not enough to live by the teachings of Jesus; one must also accept Jesus as a part of the *Holy Trinity* (three manifestations of God) and believe that he died to redeem humanity. Only in this way could one be judged worthy to ascend to Heaven after death.

Atonement

Christian doctrine teaches that all people are born in sin, sharing the sins of Adam and Eve, the first humans of Biblical myth. Because of this *original sin*, all people are separated from God, and cannot redeem themselves. The Virgin Mary (the mother of Jesus) is said to be the only person ever to be born free of original sin.

It is believed that Jesus sacrificed himself to make amends for original sin. *Atonement* is the reconciliation between God and his people, made possible by Jesus' death. Jesus taught people what they must do to redeem themselves, and gave his life so they would have an opportunity for redemption.

The Holy Trinity

The doctrine of the Holy Trinity states that there is only one God, but God is also three entities the Father, Son, and Holy Spirit who are united in one substance or being.

Jesus' disciples were Jews and worshipped their one God, Yahweh. Christianity diverged from Judaism in its belief that Jesus was Yahweh's son, and Yahweh's manifestation on Earth. Thus Christians can pray to God as Yahweh in the form of Jesus.

The Holy Trinity compares the Christian conception of God with the concept of a source, a coming forth, and a return.

Divisions of Christianity

Early Christianity eventually developed into three major branches: the Roman Catholic Church, the Eastern Orthodox Church, and the Protestant Church.

The Roman Catholic Church

The Roman Catholic Church is under the authority of the Pope, its highest religious official.
- The Pope is said to be the successor to Saint Peter, the founder of the Christian Church.
- Roman Catholics consider the Pope to be infallible regarding matters of faith and morality. The Pope may have erroneous views on other subjects, such as politics

or history, but his religious opinions and his pronouncements are believed to be the will of God.
- The Catholic Church practices seven rituals instituted by Jesus as ways one's faith is affirmed and one's life path dedicated and strengthened. These seven sacraments are baptism, confirmation, matrimony, holy orders for clergy, penance, the Eucharist, and Anointing of the Sick, or last rites.
- Many sacraments are performed only once in a person's life, while penance and the Eucharist occur regularly throughout one's life. Penance requires that a person confess all his or her sins to a priest and then pray or perform some other task in reparation, to earn God's forgiveness. In the sacrament of the Eucharist, or Holy Communion, the priest re-enacts Jesus Christ's last supper with his apostles. Bread and wine are consecrated to become representative of the body and blood of Christ, and then distributed to the congregation members for spiritual nourishment.

The Eastern Orthodox Church
- The Eastern Orthodox Church officially broke away from the Roman Catholic Church in 1054. It predominates in Eastern European countries such as Albania, Bulgaria, Greece, Romania, and Russia.
- The Eastern Orthodox Church administers the same seven sacraments as the Roman Catholic Church.
- There is no supreme and infallible religious official, like the Catholic Pope. Spiritual guidance and decisions on religious issues are provided by a consensus of bishops. This Church believes that the Holy Spirit guides and protects the spirituality of Christians, so a human leader is not necessary.
- Bishops meet regularly in councils to resolve questions of doctrine. They address the interpretation of existing doctrines, rather than instituting new doctrines.
- There is less separateness among members of this Church, and each member's salvation is tied to all others within the Church. The feeling of community may be stronger, as the members of the Church are considered to be its voice and its essence.

- Eastern Orthodox priests do not always follow the strict code of celibacy practiced in the Roman Catholic Church.

The Eastern Orthodox Church encourages individuals to seek union with God in this life, making this realization more prone to mysticism and mystical teachings.

The Protestant Church

Protestantism began as a movement to reform the Christian church in the 16th century, resulting in the Protestant Reformation. The term Protestant is applied to any Christian who is not a member of the Roman Catholic or Eastern Orthodox Churches, and is based on the religious faith of the individual.

Protestants believe that faith is first and foremost, and all else will naturally follow if one loves God and has deep, abiding faith in Him.

- The principle thrust of Protestantism rejects idolatry and all else that takes away from God. God alone should be the focus of religious worship.
- God must therefore become manifest to each individual. The Bible, God's word (called the Living Word) should speak directly to each of us, and its teachings should be applied to our daily lives.
- The hundreds of different churches in Protestantism often reflect diverse ethnic or social groups.
- The pursuit of spiritual knowledge and revelation of God's truth is an individual path for the Protestant. It can at times be a very lonely path, without the sense of community wholeness and unity that other Christian Churches offer.

Spiritual Choices and Practices

Awareness of our own spiritual needs is necessary to our happiness and fulfillment.

Religion helps most people throughout the world explore and satisfy their spiritual needs. It offers techniques of prayer and rituals for expressing our spirituality, and provides guidance and encouragement to help us on our chosen path of enlightenment.

Choosing a Religion

Most of us follow the religious traditions in which we were raised. But some of us have had little or no religious training, or found our parents religion do not answer our current spiritual needs.
- The Western world's obsession with technology, logical thinking, and materialism has left some of us with a feeling of alienation from our spiritual selves.
- Exploring and adopting an Eastern tradition, with its different values and beliefs, can sometimes help us understand and express our spirituality.
- Choosing a religion outside of one's own culture can be a form of revolt against parents or society, or it can be a crucial step in strengthening one's identity and fulfilling emotional needs.

Modern travel and communications have allowed us a greater exposure to the myriad of religions practiced throughout the world. Any religion we investigate will probably contain elements we concur with and also elements we cannot accept or feel unsure of. The practice of a single religion may vary greatly among different congregations and geographic, ethnic, or social groups. The many available choices can seem overwhelming.

- Many people, especially in the Western world, are culturally conditioned to view God as an abstract, omnipotent being, as portrayed in Judaism or Christianity.
- To someone raised in Eastern culture, the many representations of divinity found in Hinduism or Tibetan Buddhism may seem more acceptable.
- An increasingly prevalent theory suggests that all religions are simply facets of the universal belief in Divinity. In this view, each religion developed to fit the geographical, historical and traditional values of the region of its birth.

The Benefits of Religious Faith

As we study the major religions of the world, we find many similarities:
- All religions teach that we are of divine origin.
- The true essence of Self, resides in the soul rather than the body, and it is capable of existence beyond or without the body.
- Our souls can merge with the Divine Infinity.
- Techniques of prayer and meditation help us focus on our true selves, and encourage our spiritual growth and fulfillment.
- Religions offer answers to our questions about the cause and the purpose of life and death. We are reminded that there is some power greater than ourselves, of which we are a part.
- Religions give us models of humanistic behavior, that encourage and inspire us to contribute to our communities and help those in need. Most religions promote such qualities as humility, charity, kindness and truthfulness. They also condemn behaviors which are detrimental to the community and to individuals, such as murder, lying, theft, and greed.
- Shared rituals and worship services give practitioners a sense of belonging.

Religions are like the different rays of a single light, separated into all its component colors as it passes through a prism. As worshipers of one specific faith, we may bask in our own ray of color, and mistakenly believe that we know the full light.

Take time to identify your spiritual needs and explore your choices. If you have drifted away from the religious tradition of your family, you may want to try it again, as your needs have probably changed over time. You may find some ideas or practices that help you in your spiritual quest, without adopting the entire religion Only you can decide how best to fulfill your own spiritual needs.

A path of healthful and moderate living ensures progressive advancement towards enlightenment. There is no need for renunciation, deprivation or extremes of any kind.

Practices to Strengthen Spirituality

There are thousands of exercises and methods for finding or acknowledging the Spirit self. They are usually designed to strengthen the bond between the individual spirit and the Divine Spirit or God. Most of these practices were first developed as religious rituals or prayers. They may be performed as part of a religious devotion, used alone, or in combination with other spiritual practices.

Yoga

The Indian sage Patanjali refined the techniques of yoga and compiled them in a treatise in the second century AD. Yoga is a Hindu discipline which promotes unity of body and mind. Certain physical postures and breathing patterns are used in conjunction with intense concentration and meditation. Eventually a state of *Samadhi*, or total absorption, is reached.

There are many different forms of yoga. Some focus on physical postures, while others concentrate on elevating the mind into the realm of the spirit.
- *Jnana* yoga uses techniques of study and contemplation to develop spiritual wisdom.
- *Raja* yoga, "the Royal Road," involves the practice of austerities, selfless actions, and meditation.

- *Bhakti* yoga is centered upon love and devotion to God. This love is manifested in selfless action, prayer, contemplation, and chanting of the name of God.

Meditations

The purpose of the meditation is to empty the mind of random thoughts, so it can become open to awareness of God, which is beyond thought.

The mind is very powerful. It determines how we perceive events. It is constantly busy with wonderful ideas and fascinating perceptions. However, it also creates worries and distractions which block out the communications of the spirit. We worry that we will become poor or ill, lose our loved ones, or be lonely.

This power of the mind is the reason why spiritual exercises are necessary, and always include some method to still the mind's activity.
- A quiet mind allows us to return our thoughts to God, the creative principle behind all things we are attached to.
- Instead of being dependent on external forces such as material wealth, beauty, good luck and affection of others, we can come to know God within ourselves, and rely on God for our happiness.

Mantras and Sacred Words

Some meditations use mantras (words and sounds) chanted aloud to achieve a higher consciousness. Even as little children, we are fascinated with the sound and power of words. We are especially interested in magic words; that make things happen.

As a child cries, its mother appears with nourishment, love, and comfort. We read stories in which doors open magically, and transformations occur through the sound of magic words.

We learn in the Bible and other scriptures that the Word was with God and that the Word was the beginning of everything.

Mantras are simply certain words or sounds that carry a special vibration. The vibration released when one chants a specific mantra creates certain responses.

We often think of mantras only as exotic sounds from foreign tongues. But even in our own language we can easily demonstrate the power of words.
- Angry words repeated over and over will soon erode one's self-confidence and incentive.
- Positive and loving words will nurture the person, and help to uncover talents and determination.

Chanting the names of God or praising Spirit will engender subtle transformations, from calming the fears of the mind to opening the heart which unveils the light within us.

- Mantras are often taken from sacred languages such as Sanskrit or Aramaic (the common root language of Hebrew and Arabic), because it is believed that the abundance of open vowels (*a* and *o*) in those languages creates a vibration helpful to stilling the mind and opening the heart.
- However, we can create our own mantras with any positive image, word or sound that feels appropriate, or any name of God that we find meaningful.
- A mantra can be repeated at a whisper or more loudly. The sound vibrations not only have an effect on our mouth, tongue and lips, but also reverberate in the ear. If done in a group, these vibrations can be very powerful.

Chanting or repeating a mantra is not meant to create magical changes, but simply to soothe and open the mind so our own Universal Self can be more easily contacted.

Spiritual Healing

The force of God within us can help us to heal ourselves in body and mind.

The Power of God

If we accept that we each have a spiritual Self, then we must realize that this God force is not limited to our heart or brain or any other physical body part, but extends into each and every one of our cells.
- Our spiritual Self is everywhere within us, and it is also part of the infinite and immeasurable God.
- Therefore we can use our own spirit to draw upon the universal store of health and wellness, to strengthen and even heal ourselves.
- The universe vibrates with life. Similarly we are vibrant with life: each cell within us is vibrant with life. If any one cell or group of cells sickens, we can renew them with life-force by using our spiritual power.

Aligning Our Spiritual Energy

It is true that we do become tired, ill, and depleted of energy. This happens because we sometimes act in opposition to the natural flow of energy. We create friction and tension in our own lives. This is clearly the case when we become sick due to anxious thoughts, worries, or extreme stress. Our minds often lead us astray from our spiritual truth, causing our spirits to become ill at ease and dis-harmonious, and our bodies to become diseased.

However, simple techniques can help us realign our energy and strengthen ourselves:
- Deep breathing and relaxation exercises are invaluable.
- We must become aware of the natural rhythms around us, and relax our breath and very being into those rhythms. We find natural rhythms everywhere: the waves of the oceans, the songs of frogs or crickets at dusk, a water fountain, rain, our own heartbeat, and any other vibration of the natural world.

- We must also practice awareness of the life-force inherent in all things.
- Awareness of our own life-force comes from visualizing and concentrating on our centers of energy (or *chakras*, in the study of yoga): the navel, the solar plexus, the heart, the throat, the Spirit center between the eyebrows, and the crown center at the top of the head. While concentrating on the centers of energy, repeat their corresponding affirmations (working up from the navel center): I create, I live, I love, I speak, I am, I bless.
- In every spiritual tradition in the world, these centers of energy have been used (though often subconsciously) as focal points for prayer and meditation.
- Very potent spiritual healing is realized by focusing one's intent upon the chosen energy center, and visualizing a strong white light and powerful healing energy there.
- Complete charts of the body's energy centers and their corresponding colors for visualizations are available in many books on yoga or meditation, and can be taught by most yoga teachers.
- One healing technique is done by visualizing that one is inhaling and exhaling a white light. The white light is the divine force that can be directed through the energy centers, the spinal column or even over the entire body like a fountain of health and wellness. It is interesting to note that many religions use a blinding white light as one representation of God.
- Such powerful visualizations, practiced regularly, can bring great calmness, vitality, balance, harmony, and mental and spiritual strength.

Healing
Three practical steps to change disease to health:
- Help others so that you may be healed. This act of helping others takes your mind off your personal illusions of illness.
- Give thanks, as though healing has already happened. This will increase your faith. You must believe that you will heal. But how do you get this faith? You simply give energy to the results by visualizing them as having already occurred. If you give thanks and see something

as already happening, this allows faith to go with your affirmations. Your faith will allow you to make the leap into your new reality.
- Call forth God. Affirm that "I am healed now." Whatever you say after "I am" is sent directly into the sub-conscious and is very powerful.

Spiritual Decision

Living means having to make major decisions, about everything from buying a house to choosing a religion. Even not deciding is actually a decision to remain unchanged in your current situation. Evaluating options based on incomplete information and changing emotions can lead to bad decisions. Accessing your higher wisdom will help you find the best solution.

Techniques for Spiritual Decision Making

Get in a relaxed, comfortable sitting position and still your mind. Silently state the problem that you face, and ask what you need to do to take the next step forward. Listen to that small voice within. Without thinking about it, write down whatever you are given as the next step forward. If you have the courage to follow the instructions from your higher self, your life will unfold perfectly.

But how do you know if what you write comes from God or somewhere else? There are four characteristics that indicate that the answer came from God rather than ego. If your answer does not have the following four characteristics, try again until you get an answer that fits.

Answers from God

1. Does the answer have the ring of truth? Does it feel like the right thing to do?

2. Is it a brief answer? A short, simple answer is more likely to come from God, while a long complicated answer is more likely to come from ego.

3. Does the answer show the qualities of higher wisdom? Qualities such as love, forgiveness, kindness, and understanding are likely to come from God.

4. Does the answer give you a sense of upliftment? Your ego may create an answer that is a put-down to yourself or someone else. Destructive and negative answers do not come from God.

CHAPTER 4
SPIRITUAL FULFILLMENT

> *"A human being is a part of the whole called by us universe. A part limited in time and space. He experiences himself, his thoughts and feelings as something separate from the rest – a kind of optical delusion of his consciousness. This delusion is a kind of prison for us. Our task must be to free ourselves from this prison."*
>
> *–Albert Einstein*

Overview of Chapter

The highest experience of fulfillment in life is to realize our direct connection with the divine. Mystical teachings of all major religions prescribe various ways to achieve this direct connection. Neither logical nor emotional, this connection requires a leap beyond everyday normal knowing. It requires the realization that we are more than just our bodies and our minds. We are actually children of God, an outflowing of the Divine God. As we learn more about spiritual truth, we are bound less by the physical and mental laws of man and more by the laws of God. Physical and mental laws no longer hold their former degree of power over us. We are now able to cut through the complexities of human life and go directly to the center of spiritual existence.

Looking within to find the key to Self is like penetrating a maze to find its center. Questions may only lead to more questions. Yet with a pure heart and clear vision, one can find the center of the maze, the Reality of the Self, a sense of wholeness and belonging, the key to answering all questions, the still quiet place within, where one can truly see and hear and know. How are we to acquire this pure heart and clear vision?

In this chapter you are given the priceless opportunity to understand the spiritual nature of life. You will learn to train your mind to let go of old belief systems that no longer work. This chapter's lessons can be an agent of inner healing and guide you to your true identity.

Spiritual Meditations

This chapter on spirituality is extremely potent. The mind is powerful; it controls the body and creates health and happiness. God is even more powerful than either the mind or body; it is the ultimate source of all power. A spiritual life is absolutely necessary for psychological and physical health.

It is difficult to logically explain spiritual wisdom because spiritual consciousness requires an understanding beyond logic. Spirituality exists on a higher plane of awareness than the mechanical thinking of the mind. Therefore, a different type of training is necessary. Spiritual principles taught in this chapter may at first seem illogical or even incorrect. However, they will be catalysts for us to grow beyond conditioning and logic into awareness of spiritual truth.

Almost all of the world's spiritual masters and teachers have said that meditation is the way to peace, joy and spiritual illumination. So the purpose of these meditative spiritual exercises is training to go beyond the limitations of our mind and into an alignment with the spiritual view of Reality. We normally live our life in an illusion, with a sense of separation from God. We each usually become mesmerized by the events of everyday life and forget our spiritual nature. The meditations assist in awakening us from life's hypnotic trance, which is so powerful that we need some type of spiritual meditation on a daily basis. Although there are rare cases of spontaneous alignment, most of us must learn some formal method to free us from our trance.

In this series of fifty-two spiritual meditations, we simply focus our whole attention on a spiritual concept. At the same time, we remain receptive to the flow of information coming to us from infinite God. We accomplish this by reading about the theme of the week. Sitting in regularly-scheduled meditations and contemplating the specific weekly concept, all the while listening for that still small spiritual voice within us. If distracting thoughts come to your mind – as they surely will – acknowledge them briefly but remain unattached, and return to the theme of the week.

The meditations provided in this chapter are designed to facilitate a profound spiritual growth within one year. The meditations are non-sectarian and use the general name "God." However, you may substitute other names such as Spirit, Christ, The Great I Am, The Eternal All-Powerful, Allah, etc.

In this section there are a total of fifty-two spiritual meditations. Study each for an entire week. Choose a day of the week, possibly Saturday or Sunday, to begin a new spiritual meditation. Try to consciously practice the spiritual meditation twice every day, but don't "beat yourself up" if you miss some days. Generally about ten minutes is sufficient. The meditations are to be done in order. Don't skip any. Whatever posture you assume is okay. Most people prefer sitting in a comfortable position. Noises are very distracting, so choose a quiet place and ensure that you will not be disturbed. The preferred time for the first daily spiritual meditation is as soon as possible after awakening in the morning. Do the repetition of the spiritual meditation any time you choose. Also throughout the day, whenever you have an opportunity, think about the week's meditation.

Begin by reading everything in the weekly spiritual meditation, and then concentrate on the statement in the box for five minutes with your eyes closed. Say this statement a number of times to yourself, and consider how it applies to your life and the people and things around you.

Understanding the truth of God requires embracing a larger perspective than just logic. You don't have to understand the statements, just reflect on them during the week. Certain key concepts are repeated in various ways during the course of the year.

One Year Spiritual Training

Exercise for Week 1 (Reality)

Each person views the world through his own perspective. As though each individual wears filtered glasses with different color filters, and therefore, reports seeing different colored objects.

The problem is that we almost never remove our personal filters, and consequently we have a distorted viewpoint of Reality. An example of this is to look at a tree and note our observation. We might see it as a large umbrella that provides shade from the sun. Other individuals might see a log to turn into lumber. Others might see a source of beautiful flowers, tasty nuts, leaves to rake, etc. Birds may consider the tree their home, and termites may consider it their food. The true Reality is all of the above and much more!

> "The world I see is only a very small part of total Reality."

Once we see one thing differently, we then have the ability to begin seeing yet other things differently. We will understand that there are different ways to perceive the world. While our five senses give us information, we interpret this information in various ways. We give the meaning to what is there. In the past we have chosen to focus on those things that our conditioned mind dictates. Now we begin to recognize that the reality we see is only a very small part of total Reality.

Exercise for Week 2 *(Reality)*

We generally think dreams occur only at night when we are sleeping. In fact dreams also take place during the day. We actually see things as if viewed through a filter, distorting our perception of Reality and limiting our ability to perceive the world. Reality is much more than what we believe we see or touch in the external world. This week's spiritual meditation will help us realize that we see "through a glass darkly."

Certain thoughts remind us we are dreaming instead of being focused in Reality. They are there to remind us that there are other ways to understand our experience.

Replace dream thoughts of fear, separation, lack and limitation with Reality thoughts of love, unity, and abundance.

> **"What I see is distorted by my dream thoughts."**

Our internal filter distorts our perception of experience. This filter is created by our unconscious mind. Most people are unaware of how to control the unconscious mind. By repeating this spiritual meditation during the week, we can begin to see particular events in our life from a different perspective.

Exercise for Week 3   (*Reality*)

The human condition can seem like one problem after another. Our freedom from needless pain and suffering in life depends on our becoming awakened from illusion. Perception is a choice; we can consciously choose to focus on pain and suffering, or we can choose to focus on joy and happiness. We can choose to transform negative and dysfunctional beliefs into more positive ones that work for us.

> **"Liberation from illusion brings joy and happiness."**

Some people think that suffering is the way to grow, but it does not bring us closer to God. Understanding the truth of our being brings liberation and lasting peace and joy and happiness. This liberation can come only from our conscious choice to be free.

The challenges and conflicts of the illusionary outer world cannot bring lasting happiness. We may have noticed that the goals set by our old conditioned mind do not bring lasting happiness. Successful completion of our individual goals may bring fleeting happiness, but we quickly seek a new and more difficult goal to accomplish. Only liberation from illusion brings enduring happiness.

Conflicts and suffering offer us opportunities to choose to transcend the illusions. Many people awaken after a period of intense suffering. At these times of pain our choices become more obvious. Conscious choice for liberation often follows when we feel that we can't or won't take any more suffering.

Exercise for Week 4   (*Reality*)

Sometimes it seems we are controlled by life's events. It seems like all we can do is react. The onslaught of happenings can eventually overwhelm us. It takes courage to realize that we can learn to see life's challenges in a different way. Our mechanical mind tells us one thing, but a small voice deep within us says that we can indeed see things differently. It says that we are the masters of our destiny and do have a choice.

> "I can change my perception and choose joy and happiness."

We have a variety of thought systems with which to experience life. We can choose separation, fear, lack and limitation. Or we can choose love, harmony, abundance and peace.

This week when you think of something negative, try to observe it from another viewpoint.

Exercise for Week 5   (*Reality*)

Holding on to outdated viewpoints of life limits our ability to realize our higher Self. By removing our old limiting ideas, we can expand our consciousness to include a more comprehensive understanding of life. What more is the purpose of life than growing from infancy into adulthood and progressively seeing things more fully?

> "I am committed to growing, and will release my outdated concepts about life."

Once we can see an expanded reality in one area of our life, it becomes easier to see an expanded reality in other parts of our life. This is because we begin to understand that our preconceived ideas about things are only a small portion of the total picture. We soon understand that we can withhold initial judgments about initial perceptions and thereby observe a larger Reality. This encourages us to continue to awaken from our sleep and to know the truth even more fully.

Exercise for Week 6   (Reality)

It is impossible to understand infinite God with our finite, logical minds. Sometimes certain events occur repeatedly and we can not understand the reasons. Some people are married and divorced a number of times to the same type of spouse. Others held a series of similar jobs, which ended quickly. These types of events continue to occur until we finally learn the lessons that we are meant to learn from the experience.

Occasionally seemly dreadful things happen and we ask why these things happen to us. We would much prefer only pleasant events to occur. Why do "bad" things happen? And why do they continue to happen? If everything in life was picture perfect we would never learn anything. The various circumstances we confront during routine living are opportunities to learn to see Reality.

> "All events hold lessons of truth."

We have taken form in human bodies to learn truths necessary to the evolution of our spiritual beings. The specific events we experience are not as important as the truths that we learn from them. Try to consider all events as opportunities to learn and to grow. Whenever faced with challenges of any kind, be thankful for the opportunity to learn and grow. Don't reject the powerful lessons that we can learn from all life's events, whether positively or negatively perceived.

Exercise for Week 7 *(I am)*

Most of the world's spiritual teachers agree that all things were made by the one infinite God. They believe that human life was created in the image and likeness of God. Our humanness is the life given to us by God. We were created by God and therefore live in relation with God.

> "I come from God."

God did not create us just to abandon us. We maintain relationship with God. When we don't see this truth, we are living in a dream. Our true being is in the image and likeness of God. We are an outpouring of God.

Exercise for Week 8 *(I am)*

On occasion we believe that our thoughts or actions do not measure up to some idea we might have about successful living. These perceived imperfections then produce feelings of sin and guilt within us. This guilt in turn can lead to low self-esteem or self-punishing behavior.

Our old thoughts of being not good enough, or of somehow lacking, only occur due to our conditioning. In fact God made us perfect, in Its image, and gave us the choice to confirm or deny this perfection. Unfortunately, most of humanity denies its perfection. Nevertheless, the truth of our being is always within us. It is only necessary to take off the false blinders of our old conditioning, in order to recognize our kinship to God.

> "I am perfect now, just as God created me."

Once we really learn this week's spiritual meditation we will be free of the world's illusions of our imperfections. There will be nothing in us that needs fixing. Awareness of our source will free us from sickness and disease. Knowing our perfect being will free us from the world's illusions of lack and limitations. We were created as part of the perfect God, and are perfect as such.

Exercise for Week 9 (*I am*)

Success comes from being steadfast and not quitting. In today's busy world, so many demands are made upon our time and energies that we often feel almost overwhelmed. We feel that we have no control over our lives. But we can decide to set aside a few minutes twice a day, during which we can begin to take charge of our lives. If we practice our spiritual meditation on a regular daily schedule, we will be successful. All those who truly want to know and remember their true identity will be motivated to continue and ultimately succeed.

> "I remain steadfast in my desire
> to remember my true identity."

For most of us this is an important element of spiritual growth. To have a strong desire and be steadfast in that desire will enable us to complete any task. It will assist us in our leap of awareness from the material to the spiritual plane. It will help us remember our true nature as part of God. This is the most freeing experience in the world. It brings us peace and happiness.

Exercise for Week 10 (*I am*)

When we experience fear, it means that we see ourselves separately, as body or mind and not as part of God. When we remember our true nature as more than our body and our mind, we are not afraid. We are part of God and nothing can harm our true identity.

> "I remember my true identity and
> do not fear the world's illusions."

God is infinite and all-powerful. It can not be harmed by anything that man or nature does. When we remember that we are more than simply our mind and body, our fear will lose its power.

Exercise for Week 11   (I am)

We generally ignore the cycles of change that occur in our lives. An example of changing cycles can be seen in the egg that hatches into a caterpillar. This caterpillar spends its life eating large quantities of plant matter necessary for its growth. The larva's life purpose is to feed upon vegetation and grow. This is like the unconscious portion of man's life during which he consumes elements of the material world.

Eventually the caterpillar spins a cocoon spending this phase of its life in this pupal case in quiet metamorphous. This is like the quiet time a man spends when he is devoted to contemplating the world of illusion and the world of God.

Finally a butterfly emerges from the cocoon. The beautiful butterfly no longer eats plant matter, but now visits fragrant flowers and drinks their sweet nectar. This compares to man's enlightenment after he realizes his connection with God when his existence miraculously changes.

> "I am more than my body. I am part of God."

Our body also developed through cycles. It began as a sperm and egg that combined to form a one cell animal in our mother's womb. Was that really us? Once it was a crying baby. Was that really us? Do we have the same thoughts today? Scientists tell us that each molecule in our body is replaced every few years. Where are we?

As we grow older we continue to change. Who are we? The only answer is, that as part of God, we are more than those things.

Exercise for Week 12 *(I am)*

We don't have to travel to mountain tops or holy places to communicate with God. God is always within us, closer than our hands and feet. When we don't feel God within, we are just not alert to its presence. But God is still there. It is like radio waves that surround us, but that we can't hear unless we use a radio to tune in to one particular wave and tune out the rest of the signals. We need to "tune us" to God, and tune out other distractions.

> **"God is forever with me, closer than my own hands and feet."**

At the center of our being God has incarnated itself. God is part of our very core. We all share the same God. God has given us individual outward expressions in material form. But in our very core we are the infinite God. Our true Self is part of the God.

Exercise for Week 13 *(I am)*

Honor yourself acknowledging your true identity as part and parcel of the unlimited God. Wherever you are, God is. Accept your true nature and joy, and freedom becomes your birthright.

> **"My true identity is part of the unlimited God."**

We will never die because our true Self is part of God. The body and mind exist in time and will eventually age, decay and die. God exists beyond the concept of time. It exists in the infinite here and now. It always existed and always will exist. Our real identity as a part of that infinite God is ageless.

Exercise for Week 14   *(One God)*

God is the only power and the only law. This may seem confusing since each of the various belief systems, are filled with different laws and traditions. The realized person is not bound by the millions of man-made laws. These are set up for those who don't yet recognize their true nature as being part of God. We invented them ourselves in an attempt to protect ourselves from the multiple worldly powers. As long as we believe in worldly powers they will control us. Once we realize that we are not bound by these man-made laws, we will experience a tremendous sense of freedom.

> "There is only one God, one power, one law."

It is not possible for the one infinite, perfect God to be divided against itself. The only laws are the laws of God. All other laws come from the human mind. Freedom is recognizing that we do not need to obey all the beliefs and rules drilled into us from the first moment of our birth. Though they were necessary in our earlier, formative years, these old rules now enslave us. We may no longer reach for our mother's hand before we cross the street, but there are still thousands of apparently "logical rules" that interfere with our awareness of the one true power.

Exercise for Week 15   *(One God)*

This week we will learn that God is everywhere that it is realized. Wherever we accept the presence of God, it is!

> "There is only one God and It is everywhere."

Look slowly around the room, and focus attention on various items, and repeat this spiritual meditation. God is even in the chair, the desk, the door, etc. Affirm that God is in every item that comes into our awareness. God is literally within every thing that we can perceive.

Apply this week's spiritual meditation periodically throughout the day. Repeat it whenever we have a few free moments.

Exercise for Week 16 (*One God*)

Sitting in a room with drawn curtains in complete darkness, we might feel alone and afraid. We may feel the pain and suffering of human existence. But throw open those curtains, and the room is flooded with light. The warm loving light that has been within us since the beginning is revealed. It shines forth as our experience of the infinite God. The white light of God will sweep away the terrors of darkness. Darkness cannot survive when illuminated by this light. So when light comes, darkness loses its appearance of Reality. Darkness does not exist except as the absence of light. The light of God brings its awareness of who and what we are. We are part of God and God is part of us.

> **"God is part of me and I am part of God."**

When light enters a room there is still a shadow that accompanies it. Just as we were afraid of the dark, it's also natural to fear the shadows. Most people spend their lives fighting their shadow selves. Instead of fighting throw open those curtains still wider flooding the room with more of the blinding light of God. This omnipresent light dissipates the shadows from even the farthest corners of our mind.

Exercise for Week 17   (*Love*)

If we view ourselves as separate from God, we also feel separate from other humans. When we realize we are part of God, we view other humans as part of us. This enables us to perceive them differently – on a higher level, and acknowledge our oneness. We realize that getting angry at others is the same as getting angry at ourselves. Loving others is the same as loving ourselves.

The love of God varies greatly from the conditional love of the material world. The love of God has no degrees or limits, and is unchanging and forever. It is accepting and non-judging. This love actually comprises who you are.

> **"I feel the love of God."**

When you feel the love of God you will see the entire world through new loving eyes. Your fresh vision is very different from the fearful and angry world of your past. This world you see now is free from danger, hatreds, pain, suffering, separation, failure, conflict and strife of the world you once knew.

Exercise for Week 18 (*Trust*)

Feelings of loneliness, suffering and depression come from one's sense of separation from God. Unity with God instantly restores peace and happiness. The light of God illuminates the darkness. Just as there can be no darkness where there is light, there is no suffering when we realize God.

> "God protects and watches over me."

God is perfect, and acceptance of this perfect God will cure all our suffering and depression. God protects us in all circumstances. We have nothing to fear because God is our strength, and its strength is infinite. If we fear something, it shows that we are attempting to rely upon our own strength and not upon the strength of God. God sustains our very life; without God, we could accomplish nothing. God is all-powerful; there is nothing God cannot do. We need only ask God for direction. Turn over all worries and problems to the all-powerful God that watches over and protects us.

Exercise for Week 19 *(Error)*

Let us never forget who we truly are. We are one with God, and not under the power of the illusory material world. Our kingdom is not of this world of illusion, but of the world of truth. Once we recognize this, we no longer suffer from loss and limitation. If we do suffer, it is because we did not turn over our problems to the all-powerful God. Instead we remain lost in illusion.

> "I take full responsibility for what I think and feel."

If we suffer from pain, either mental or physical, it is because we choose to suffer. We blame others instead of taking responsibility for our not turning over the pain to God. Pain exists only in the illusionary world where our negative thoughts and resistance bring forth suffering. Suffering is not possible when we elect to live in the truth, instead of the material world. Remember, we choose for ourselves whether to be sad or glad.

Exercise for Week 20 *(Error)*

Suffering, lack and limitation grow from desiring for things to be different from the way they are. Sometimes we are able to see that we want things which we believe will eventually bring us happiness. But when we finally achieve these things, we get only a fleeting kind of happiness. Soon we desire new and better things. We still don't get the lasting happiness which we so long for. Our old mind soon desires bigger and better things.

> "I choose to be free from suffering."

Only God can bring lasting happiness. God is responsible for the universe, and made it perfectly and without error. Any error exists only in our minds when we think things should be different from what they are. Pain and suffering are an illusion of the mind.

Exercise for Week 21 *(Error)*

We cannot cure lack, limitation and suffering. It does not truly exist. All we can do is recognize that the appearance of suffering is not real. The choice between joy and suffering is ours. It's our dream. We can decide!

> "I choose the joy of God instead
> of the suffering of illusions."

There is no lack or limitation to fight against. You don't overcome suffering by overpowering anything, but by remembering that there is no real power in the illusion of suffering. Suffering has only the power of the belief that you give to its appearance. Choose joy instead and the suffering disappears, much like darkness disappears.

Exercise for Week 22 (Error)

Let us not be fooled by the rewards of the material world. Millions of dollars in the bank do not bring us any closer to God than someone who may not even have a bank account. The true and lasting demonstrations of abundance, peace, and happiness are internal, not external. The true riches come from God and have nothing to do with more money, a bigger car, or a higher position.

> **"God gives me life and releases me from all illusion."**

Most people believe that there are two powers in the Universe. One is the power of the material world, and the other is the power of God. But in fact only the power of God exists. The material power is only illusion created by our dream thoughts.

The belief in two powers comes from the misperception of a power separate and apart from the One God. The belief in two powers presents itself as lack, limitation, sin, separation, sickness and death. These states were not created by God, but dreamed by the mind of man. Our realization of the emptiness of what we see in the material world is the only way to dissolve this illusion. Awaken and see through it!

Exercise for Week 23   (*Error*)

As humans, we believe we were created involuntarily and can be destroyed at any time, without our consent. We are like frightened children who hear a ghost story and look everywhere for the imaginary ghost. Like children, we see life as filled with danger, and seek help wherever we can find it. But the human help we find is temporary at best, and soon new ghosts frighten us.

> "Fear no longer controls me."

Fear means you see yourself as a limited being controlled by unpredictable worldly illusions. But you are much more than a limited mind and body. The infinite God did not create you to forever suffer in fear and limitation. God created you with the free choice to see yourself as much more than the physical Self. As your Reality expands to more fully understand your true eminence, your fears drop away. The gruesome ghost stories no longer control your reactions.

Exercise for Week 24   (*Error*)

When we are angry and think about attacking others, we do it from a state of fear. We believe in some threat, become afraid, and attack the object of our fear. Attack stems from our fear that we will be hurt by some force. We believe that we need to defend ourselves against that force.

When we remember our true identity we know that there is but one power and others' thoughts of attack cannot hurt us. Let us behold the One God in everyone that we encounter. When we go to work, the grocery store, the restaurant, let us remember that God is in everyone. Whomever we meet, let us recognize God within them.

> **"I replace thoughts of fear and attack with thoughts of love."**

Attacking others is really attacking ourselves because we are all one in God. Loving others is really loving ourselves. Let us disregard the appearance of fear and attack, and greet people with love. Let us disregard the appearance of human identity and greet God within all beings. People will react in a positive way and reflect back to us the loving energy that we have released.

Exercise for Week 25   (*Error*)

Throughout history people have dedicated their lives to the erroneous cause of fighting evil. But God is the only power and there is nothing that needs to be resisted.

What we resist will persist. What we focus on grows in importance. When we defend ourselves we create conflict. Defense arises from fear that we are unsafe. But our true Self is one with God, and cannot be harmed. Our true Self always existed and will always exist. Our true Self is the one and only power, and no other powers can be aligned against this one power. Any other powers are just illusionary, and are only perceived as real and powerful by those who don't yet understand the truth of their being.

> "In my defenselessness is my freedom."

Our defenselessness is our safety. Carrying guns and building missiles will cause our defeat. We will spend all our time seeking to be defended from the threats of the illusionary material world, rather then learning about the true world of God. This will sow the seeds of our destruction. Strong defenses really show our weakness, because they show that we don't understand who we really are.

When we fight the appearance of evil, we create an enemy in our mind that is greater than ourselves. When we fight this appearance of evil we actually give it the strength that it did not previously have. Since we defined this evil, it has all the strength we possess ourselves. We need not attempt to change the appearance of evil into good. Instead of fighting, let us look beyond appearances to the spiritual plane, where there is only good.

Exercise for Week 26   (*Error*)

The cloudy illusions of everyday life evaporate when illuminated with truth. These illusions become insignificant and vanish in the face of spiritual truth. It is not easy to view the lack, limitation, disease, and horrors of the world and remember that they have no power. We do not understand the reason things happen as the do, but infinite God has its reasons. However, the first time that we are healed because of our belief in God, we will gain renewed faith in the power of the truth.

Our everyday confused and unsure thinking creates the errors in the way we lead our life. The spiritual truth fixes these errors and allows us to go forward free of future errors.

> "Spiritual truth will heal errors in my thinking."

Separation from the truth of the infinite God creates illusion and error. But separation is not real. Hearing and living truth will free us from confused thinking.

Exercise for Week 27 (*Error*)

It is the pleasure of God to bring us health and abundance. However we must decide to accept this gift from God and not believe in sickness and limitation. We must remember our true being. We must remember that we are not separate and apart from God, but one with God. God created everything and all that It made was good. God did not make concepts such as sickness, lack and limitation. Healing occurs when we remember that sickness has no power. The hypnotic trance of everyday life attempts to convince us of the power of sickness, but this is not truth. When we remember this truth, sickness disappears.

> "I am healed now."

A rich man does not affirm that he is not poor. Affirmations made through denial will not work, so make only positive affirmations. Don't affirm that you will get better in the future. Affirm that you are healed now. A total change in consciousness is required. Realization of our identity with the one God, is all we need.

Exercise for Week 28 (*Forgiveness*)

All evil that manifests through people has its origin in the universal carnal mind. Understanding this we can separate the individual person from the evil.

The universal carnal mind believes in two powers. It is a belief in a selfhood and a power apart from God. In the Spiritual kingdom there is only One Power and there is no evil. The only evil that exists is the impersonal evil that arises when we forget our true Self and believe in the false power of the universal carnal mind.

Error is a universal belief we have accepted as our own. We have chosen to see our lives as containing evil. Once we change that perspective, we can change our lives. We have temporarily believed that error is our personal sin. We are hypnotized; and until we awaken, we remain caught up in the errors of worldly beliefs.

The only evils and sins are those in our dark unconscious mind. The light of truth illuminates the illusion of evil and sin. We can then clearly see that it is not our personal sin but the hypnosis of the world at work. The belief in personal sin disappears when illuminated by the light of truth.

> "There is no such thing as personal evil or personal sin."

Don't personalize evil by believing that individuals are evil. We can forgive others when we understand that there is no personal evil. If we punish others we stoop to operating on the same level of fear and force that they are on. Punishing individuals will not cure the hypnosis of the world. This hypnotic illusion is the real source of what we believe to be evil.

The only power is the power of the God. However, when we believe in other powers, we give them power and control over us. Only by believing in evil can these negative powers control us. Once we withdraw the belief we are free of its effect. God is infinite and all-powerful, and no other power is real.

Exercise for Week 29 (*Forgiveness*)

Belief in guilt and blame are hindrances to our own spiritual growth. Let us choose to free ourselves from either blaming others or blaming ourselves.

> "People are doing the best they can for the awareness they have."

When we remember that people are only living up to their understanding of Reality, we can forgive their trespasses because they don't know what they are doing. They are living in a hypnotic dream and are really not responsible for the actions they take.

People can't properly judge a course of action based on partial evidence. And if they don't know the truth of their being, they cannot have the complete evidence. The results will be off, but we must not condemn those who are still in the dark. We should choose compassion and forgive them as others have forgiven us.

If we see others committing an error, let us realize that their belief within their hypnotic world is the real culprit. People can only react according to the level of their understanding of the truth.

Exercise for Week 30 (*Forgiveness*)

Most of humanity does not yet see the truth. They are lost in hypnotic illusions, and this distorted viewpoint causes wrong action. We cannot pass judgment on those who don't understand. They act according to their current limited understanding of truth. If they knew better they would do better.

Don't allow the actions of others to affect your choice of action. To remain free, we must forgive those who act without knowledge of the truth.

> "I will forgive those who do not yet see the truth."

The true identity of each of us is the perfect God. Therefore we are all the same and there is truly nothing to forgive. The law of God is forgiveness, compassion and doing unto others as we would have others do unto us. No matter what others appear to be doing, forgive them.

Exercise for Week 31 (*Forgiveness*)

If we tear a sheet of paper, the two torn edges become opposites. Where one has a hill the other has a valley. Many people will look at one edge and judge it as different than the other edge. Yet it was the same sheet of paper before it was torn. Both edges were created from the same sheet of paper and were once one.

We constantly judge events and people. We consider things to be good or bad, success or failure, more or less. These are the illusions of the world as seen through a mind that perceives Reality as sets of opposites. In our growth from childhood, this concept of opposites was useful to make sense out of a confusing stream of information bombarding our consciousness. However, this view of the world gets in the way of understanding spiritual Reality.

> "I will not judge others."

When we look at another person, let's not look at his outward human appearance. Instead look beyond, to God within him, and remember that his true being is God. This week do not form negative judgments against others.

When we judge others according to the appearance they make, we will not gain freedom, but will be caught in the false illusions of life. When we stop judging others, we free ourselves from illusion. We will see Reality more clearly and understand the truth of God.

This is also our key for getting along with other people. Remember back before we began to study about God. Remember the problems we created for ourselves. Remember how we reacted to life with fear. We didn't know any better then. Today most people still don't know any better.

Exercise for Week 32 (*Forgiveness*)

Our reluctance to forgive is an obstacle to our spiritual growth. We deserve to be free of the limitations and baggage that came with holding grudges. Ask your mind to step back and review without judgment. Ask God to come forth and teach you the peace and harmony in forgiveness.

When we see others as wrong, then we judge. As soon as we see others as operating under the perfect law of God, we also release ourselves from judgment. We thus free ourselves to operate from the higher spiritual law.

> **"Forgiveness will bring me closer to God."**

It is true in life that what we sow determines what we reap; we receive the same thing that we give. When we judge others we invite judgment from others. Our attitude will bring more negative occurrences, which will lead to even more judgment. When we sow forgiveness, we will reap peace of mind which will bring us closer to God. When we forgive others we are also forgiving ourselves. When we no longer judge others we no longer judge ourselves.

Exercise for Week 33 (*Forgiveness*)

We can forgive and undo our past as if it never occurred. In fact the past never really occurred, because we saw it through a judgmental filter. We selectively remember events. We change the meaning and color the results.

We need not suffer for this false past. Let us cut loose our anchor to the past. The false past need not control our present. It doesn't matter what sins we think we have committed. Let's forgive ourselves now and let go of our past.

> "I forgive myself and release my past."

It is not your sin or wrong thinking that has caused your suffering. Suffering did not begin in you, so don't judge yourself. Suffering and error are impersonal, so forgive yourself for everything you imagined you did wrong. Error is just an illusion that disappears when you remember the infinite positive power of the God.

Exercise for Week 34 (*Love-Peace*)

This week we will claim the heritage that is our birth right, the peace of God. We have the right to be released from the suffering and ignorance of the material world. We can be assured that God will bring us the peace and prosperity we deserve.

> "God, let me see problems differently and enter into peace."

There often seem to be thousands of problems assaulting us. Let's step back and realize the spiritual peace that will allow our trials to evaporate into the nothingness from which they came. Seek this peace whenever the troubles of the material world encroach on your inner peace.

It's difficult to solve problems on the level of the problem. A better solution is to go beyond these problems into the Reality of God which is our true being. At this level all our problems have already been solved by God. We need only go beyond the worldly methods to see that our problems have, in Reality, been solved. The peace that we are entitled to has only been masked by problems we assumed were insurmountable.

Exercise for Week 35 (*Love-Peace*)

It has been written: "My peace I give unto thee: not as the world giveth." This refers to the love and peace that are beyond the logical concepts of the material world. It is a higher peace than that afforded by the pleasures of the mind and body.

> "The love and peace of God are within me."

Rejoining our true nature of God allows love and peace to flow through us. Rejoining allows us to undo anything in our past, as if it had never occurred. In truth it never did actually occur. It was only our reaction to specific events, or dreams. The love and peace were always within us. Even when we dreamed about attacking others, the truth within us was always of love.

Exercise for Week 36 (*Love-Peace*)

We are not alone in the limited Self that our mind created. Instead we are part of God, and God feeds us the love that we desire. The Self that our past conditioning created does not exist except in our mind. We created this limited Self, and now we are expending most of our energy in sustaining it. But this Self does not bring us love and peace. Instead it brings us separation and worries. We may have noticed that all the goals that our old mind has given us have not brought us the love and peace that we seek. The achievement of one goal is quickly replaced by the desire to achieve another. Meeting the goals of our old conditioned mind will never quell our longing for love and peace.

> "The love and peace of God nourish me."

Let's remember that we are perfect exactly as God created us. The love and peace of God are ours to have, and there is nothing we need to do but to accept this flow from God. Let's not separate ourselves off from this flow of good. Just as the branch that is cut away from the tree will wither and die, we are not alive without the flow from our God source. When we are in the flow of God, love and peace will truly nourish us.

Exercise for Week 37 (*Love-Peace*)

This very moment, the experience of peace and joy is available to us. This is not dependent on any other person or human power. From the beginning of time our dominion over our peace and joy has existed within us. However, we have allowed this domination to slowly slip away as we put our trust exclusively in human power. But we can regain our dominance right now. We can choose to receive the perfect peace and joy of God. There is no need to wait. We can receive peace and joy this very moment.

> "The perfect peace and joy of God are mine now."

God is infinitely powerful and all other power is an illusion. God is all good; evil, lack, and limitation are illusions.

Exercise for Week 38 *(Abundance)*

God answers all sincere calls. The call, however, must be for something spiritual. Only then can we be assured of an answer. It is possible that God may not be interested in giving us a new Rolls Royce automobile, etc. God will, however, give us all that we really need.

> "I need but ask and I will receive."

Seek first the God and all other things will then be given to you. We are always with God, and all that God has is ours. Once we accept this truth, God will set us free and provide a more abundant and joyful life.

Exercise for Week 39 *(Abundance)*

God is the infinite source of our supply. If we lose part or all of our material supplies, God can immediately recreate them. There is no limit to the gifts that God can create. Its powers are infinite, beyond our imagination. It can create the entire universe and even more.

> "I claim the infinite gifts of God."

All that God has is yours. It is God's good pleasure to give you the universe.

Exercise for Week 40 (*Present*)

Past events need not affect our present Self. We can break out of these historic chains at any moment that we choose.

> "I let the past and future go. I live in the present."

Barriers to our spiritual progress are our own preconceived lacks and limitations. These barriers are rooted in our past and future thoughts. These barriers include the belief that something has to be different before we can fully know God.

There is nothing in our past that needs to be overcome. We can forgive anything that happened in the past. Instead of blaming others, let's look for the hidden gift, the lesson of life. Every situation has a gift that can help us understand God better. We can know God now, regardless of our perceived past.

Planning for the future prevents us from living in the moment. In this very moment we can have the peace of God. We can know God now.

Exercise for Week 41 *(Prayer)*

It is important to give thanks for the life that we lead. It's not that God needs to hear our thanks. Rather we must remember our gratitude for the opportunity to live and grow. The practice of expressing appreciation on a regular basis offers us an immediate connection to the joy and abundance of God.

> "I thank God for the gift of life."

This week, in gratitude for life, let us lift our hearts above despair and worry, and become joyful for the gift of life. Let's celebrate our life and give thanks to the beauty of our being.

Exercise for Week 42 (*Prayer*)

This week, let's be still and listen to that quiet, small voice within us. Let's allow it to guide us. Let us quiet our usual mind chatter and listen for that voice of guidance. This will lift us above the hypnotic world and allow us to receive the guidance that we seek.

> "I quiet my mind and receive guidance from God."

God is currently doing everything for us. Our daily practice brings us to the awareness of the perfection that God is now achieving. Through prayer we can awaken to the truth that we are not now and never were alone. We are comforted and protected by our spiritual guidance.

Exercise for Week 43 (*Prayer*)

Some people believe that they can pray for a new color television and God will provide it. Others even pray for the specific model and color of the automobile they want. Some ask for more rain and some ask for less. In a war each side prays for victory. God does not answer this type of prayer. Prayers that ask for material favors from God are futile. This type of prayer comes from mental power and not of the kingdom of God. The prayers that God does answer are those of the spiritual kingdom. These prayers should be for more spiritual knowledge, or for the ability to hear and understand God better.

> "God, let me know you correctly."

You shall know the truth of yourself as a spiritual being, and this truth will set you free.

Exercise for Week 44   (*Prayer*)

All who seek the truth of God will reach it. We will not fail to know this if we really want it. All prayers asking for knowledge of the truth are answered. When we ask to know the truth of God correctly and more fully, we will receive this knowledge. God knows exactly what we need for our growth.

> "Seeking, I cannot fail to know the truth of God."

The world of form is our classroom to learn the truth. It makes available to us lessons for spiritual growth. Everything can be used as a teacher. Every circumstance can lead us to the truth.

Exercise for Week 45   (*Prayer*)

God created various ways to come into focus. One of the most powerful is the meditation called self-remembering. Our decision to use these methods of recalling our true identity is essential to our liberation.

We must slow down our thought process, quiet our racing mind, be still, and listen to the truth. The loud chatter of the world only brings confusion and lack of meaning. Let us listen to the truth of who we really are, and not base our identity on who others say we are. Let's be still and listen to the truth.

> "When I am still and listen,
> I hear the truth of God."

The place where you now stand is holy ground. You don't need to go to a church or sanctuary. Wherever you are, God is. All you need do is be still and acknowledge your true identity, created in the image of the God.

Exercise for Week 46   (*Listen*)

When we are enmeshed in human problems that seem unsolvable, let us take time out and still our mind. Let us remember our true identity as part of God. Let us relax our mind, open our awareness and listen for the directions of God.

Let's put ourselves in the hands of God, which will direct us toward the correct path for our growth.

> "I allow God to direct my life."

God is at work now, even as we are reading this. At this very moment, we have the opportunity to allow God to direct our life. Let us surrender to the love and peace of God.

One important lesson to learn in spiritual life is "Surrender to God." Surrendering is difficult because our logical mind thinks it knows better. But this week, let us disregard the logical mind. Let's surrender to God's direction for our life. God goes before us to make the crooked places straight.

Exercise for Week 47   (*Purpose*)

Our greatest purpose in life is to remember our true identity as part of God, and listen for the directions of God. God has a plan for us and we will get the opportunity to learn it. Even if we ignore God, we will continue to be given future chances.

We will remember our purpose, but occasionally we will also forget. The path to spiritual illumination is not straight up. There are both peaks and valleys in our path. Often we will forget, and think we are lost. But we will remember again and again. Our overall path is upward. We will gradually remember our purpose more and more frequently, and for longer periods.

> "I remember my purpose."

Our purpose is not to live our lives to fulfill human desires. Our purpose is not to satisfy personal goals of supply or power. Our purpose is not to achieve personal gain. No, our purpose is to allow the will of God to be performed through us.

God is served when we remember our true identity. God is not separate and apart from our identity, but part of and within each of us.

Exercise for Week 48 (*Purpose*)

Let us live more and more in conscious union with God. Everything that we need will be provided. God will draw to us the teachers and experiences that we need.

> "I live more and more in God."

Our separation from God is not real, but only an illusion. We dream that we are alone and separate, but we never really are since we are always part of God.

Once we are able to see through the illusions of the world and perceive our true oneness with God, we will never again be so lost in these illusions. We may frequently find ourselves back in these illusions, but we will remember how to get home more quickly.

The path towards freedom is sometimes obscure, and we will no doubt stumble and fall along the way. Yet the path does spiral upward. At times it may seem that our new knowledge is very fragile and easily lost. We may think we are right back where we started, but we will remember the truth again and again more and more often. Our natural state is to communicate with and abide in God. This is our enlightenment, our salvation.

Exercise for Week 49   (*Purpose*)

This week we will practice remembering God on a regular basis. Let us begin by periodically stopping whatever we are doing (within reason) and thinking about God. It need take only ten seconds, but remember God regularly. We might time our reflection with some regular event such as the chime of an hourly clock, the bark of the dog next door, etc. Remember that we are part of God and no longer alone.

Other techniques can provide a trigger in our outer awareness the same way. We might affix a small colored dot to the face of our watch so that whenever we check the time, we remember our connection with God. We could also affix the colored dot to anything that we periodically use throughout the day.

> "I remember my connection to God throughout the day."

Our attitude towards life should be to listen to the directions given by God. When we are committed to Spiritual growth with all our heart, our path will be revealed.

Exercise for Week 50   (*Healing*)

We can see the beauty and health of the true world. We can right the upside-down, crazy world of our dreams and nightmares. All we need to do is ask to know God more completely. Have faith that everything we need to know will be revealed, but remember it takes faith. Belief in God is required even at those times when our logical mind says no!

> "I am blessed and healed by the power of God."

God will never leave or forsake us. It is not necessary to live by physical beauty, strength, mental knowledge or ability. God is within us, and all that God has, we have. This realization brings all that we will ever need. If we put our faith in the power of the infinite God, we will be blessed and healed. We can truly experience heaven on earth.

Exercise for Week 51 (*One*)

This week's spiritual meditation will remind us of our true identity. God resides within us and is our true identity. To remember our higher Self is to forget who we think we are.

We are more than just a human. We are one with the infinite God that always was and always will be. The leaf of a tree is more than just a leaf. It is a leaf but it is also part of the tree. Similarly, we are unique human individuals, and are also part of eternal God. When we remember this, we need no longer be enslaved by human law. We already are the physical manifestation of God. We are in perfect union with the One God.

Let us acknowledge now that we are eternal and infinite, not limited to our mind and body. Never doubt the everlasting love of God, because we are one with that God.

> **"God and I are one."**

From time to time we will forget ourselves, and then realize that we need new guidance. When the illusions of the world close in on us, we should shut our eyes for a moment and silently reaffirm our connection to God that is within us and is part of us. Let us affirm that we and God are one, and our true nature is incorporeal, infinite being. We dwell and have our existence in God. We are not separate from God. When we acknowledge God as inseparable from ourselves, we will be blessed and healed.

Exercise for Week 52   (Teacher)

We may want to repeat the fifty-two spiritual meditations again. We may want to do them alone or with a friend. We need not be the perfect master to teach the truth. We may continue to experience times when we forget our true being. Still, we can teach what we know. This teaching illuminates the darkness of material existence in both ourselves and in others.

> **"I am a teacher of the truth."**

Teaching does not mean inflicting our words on those who don't want to hear. Instead let us teach by example through our compassionate presence, telling only those who really want to know about the truth.

Let us teach what we would learn better. But we must not charge blindly ahead and attempt to teach those who cannot yet hear. If our beliefs are still too new and fragile, they can be shattered by the world's hypnotic reaction.

We must not attempt to tell others that they are wrong in their world view. They will resist us. Trying to force the truth on others could prevent them from being able to hear it. Instead, live the life of God, demonstrating your understanding of the eternal truth. Let the light of God shine through us. When others come to us and ask our secret, then share.

But even then, share slowly. Few people can immediately conceive our jump to a greater Reality. Let's teach the truth, but don't teach beyond the ability of our student.

Let us allow God to go before us to bring light to the darkness and make the crooked places straight. God will guide us in when, whom, and how to teach.

Daily Meditations

It's said that there is a time for everything, a time to be born and a time to die. But there is more. There is a moment beyond time, a moment when you know your true identity. For many of you, that moment is now.

Remaining aware is vital to preventing disease, lack and limitation from regaining control of your experience of life. You can continue to live a life of health, happiness and abundance by regularly remembering your true identity. The hypnotic effect of life in material bodies constantly suggests that we are separate and apart from God. Periodically recall that you are one with God, and not separate and alone. This will protect you from slipping back into the hypnotic trance that most humans accept as their world view.

Begin each day celebrating your true identity and affirming the one true power in the universe. Throughout the day, remember again and again. This is the most important meditation you can do on your spiritual path.

Various methods are available to remind you of your true Self. One method is to use an hourly clock or watch chime to remind yourself to be aware. Another method uses a habitual action such as touching your head, crossing your leg, answering the phone, etc. as a reminder to be aware. almost anything you do regularly can be used as a vehicle to awaken to your true Self. Once aware repeat an exercise from this chapter or the statement shown below.

> Be silent and listen to the magnificent Universe.
> Accept God as infinite and all-powerful.
> Ask God to direct your life.
> Remain aware of your true identity, united with God.

It was with great joy that God created the world. God saw all that was made and beheld that it was very good. It is God's good pleasure to give you everything you need. It is God's good pleasure to give you the Universe.

Recovery Work

There are times when we get caught up in the stuff of life. As we accept truth more and more into our lives, we are caught up less and less. But some things will be difficult, such as loss of a job or loved one, and challenges of poor health and death. What do we do at those times when we are really feeling down and life seems to us so negative or hopeless? When times are really difficult, use one of the following meditations. Choose the one that works best for you and use it as often as necessary. Any of these may be useful to you at various times of your life.

> "God, let me see this differently."

> "I turn it all over to God."

> "I am not this problem. I am free."

> "There is a greater plan for me, and I do not understand everything."

Enneagram Resources

There are more than twenty different Enneagram books currently in print. Following are a few of our favorites.

- *Your Secret Self* by Alan Fensin and George Ryan, published by Avon Books in 1993. This book has an excellent true and false test for determining your personality.

- *The Enneagram* by Maria Beesing, Robert Nogosek and Patrick O'Leary, published by Dimension Books in 1984. This is the first Enneagram of Personality Types book ever published and it is a classic.

- *Understanding the Enneagram* by Don Riso, published by Houghton Mifflin in 1990. Don is one of the most popular Enneagram teachers and has several excellent books.

- *My Best Self* by Kathleen Hurley and Theodore Dobson published by Harper San Francisco in 1993. This book deals with Spiritual aspects of the Enneagram.

- *The Enneagram for Youth* by William Callahan S.J. published by Loyola Universith Press in 1993. This book is directed toward the counseling of young adults.

- *The Enneagram Made Easy* by Renee Baren & Elizabeth Wagele, published by Harper San Francisco in 1994. A fun and easy guide to the Enneagram.

- *Enneagram Spirituality* by Suzanne Zuercher O.S.B. published by Ave Maria Press in 1992.

About The Author

Alan Fensin worked as an electrical engineer designer on the Apollo Man on the Moon Program from 1963 through 1969. Then in 1973 he earned an MBA from Tulane University majoring in Behavior Analysis.

In 1983 he took his first seminar in the Enneagram. He believes that the Enneagram changed his life, exposing secrets about his personality that had previously limited his career.

He has taught the Enneagram and spirituality for over twelve years and has written four books on these topics including "Your Secret Self," an Enneagram book published by Avon Books.